The competitiveness of European industry

1998 Report

This report was prepared for the European Commission by

Cambridge Econometrics
Centro de Estudios Economicos Tomillo
IFO Institut für Wirtschaftsforschung
NEI Nederlands Economisch Instituut
Prometeia Calcolo srl
WIFO Österreichisches Institut für Wirtschaftsforschung

It does not, however, express the Commission's official views. Neither the Commission nor the Consultants accept liability for the consequences of actions taken on the basis of the information contained herein.

The Directorate-General "Industry" (DGIII) would like to thank Prof. R. Baldwin, P. Buigues, A. Jacquemin, Prof. D. Neven, Prof. P. Rey and A. Sapir, members of the Scientific Committee, for their comments to the report.

A great deal of additional information on the European Union is available on the internet.
It can be accessed through the Europa server (http://europa.eu.int).

Cataloguing data can be found at the end of this publication.

Luxembourg: Office for Official Publications of the European Communities, 1998

ISBN 92-828-4964-3

© European Communities, 1998
Reproduction is authorised provided the source is acknowledged.

Printed in the Netherlands on white chlorine-free paper

Table of Contents

List of abbreviations

Executive summary   1
    Competitiveness: the key to success   1
    The problem: lag in wealth and employment creation   1
    Competitive strengths and weaknesses of European manufacturing   4
    Required tailor-made policy   6

The European economy

Macroeconomic performance   9
    1. Europe's competitive position   9
    2. Factors behind the lower European standard of living   10
    3. Jobless growth: a constant feature of the European economy   11
    4. Growth and employment in market services and manufacturing   13
    5. Costs of basic services and of labour   14

Technology and innovation   17
    1. Role and types of national innovation systems   18
    2. Efficiency of public research institutions   20
    3. Information and communication technology   23
    4. Biotechnology: Europe keeps pace   26

Access to finance for European SMEs: a potential for growth and job creation   29
    1. SMEs: a potential for job creation   29
    2. Access to finance for SMEs   30
    3. High-growth SMEs: the role of risk-capital finance   31
    4. Remaining barriers   35

The European manufacturing industry

Competitiveness and sectoral development: building the links   39
    1. Outline of the analysis   39
    2. The international division of labour   40
    3. Competitive performance and industrial structure   41
    4. Factors determining industrial structure   43

Sectoral growth, employment and productivity   47
    1. Overall trends   47
    2. Growth and the creation of jobs   50
    3. Sectoral development and productivity   52
    4. Summary and conclusions   55

European industries in world markets   57
    1. Market shares and trade balances   57
    2. Competition in quality   61
    3. Further disaggregations   68
    4. Summary   70

Industrial specialisation and performance **71**
    1. Firm's strategies 71
    2. Contributions to overall economic performance 75
    3. Okun's law by type of industry 78
    4. Competitive performance 80
    5. Summary 81

Global investment and multinational firms **83**
    1. Determinants and structural impact of multinational activity 83
    2. The multinationality of Europe's leading manufacturers 84
    3. FDI and trade 86
    4. Summary 91

The competitive strengths and weaknesses of European manufacturing: Summary and conclusions **95**
    1. Industry structure and competitive performance 95
    2. Economic policy 96

List of abbreviations

AIM	Alternative Investment Market
EASDAQ	European Association of Securities Dealers Automated Quotation System
FDI	Foreign Direct Investment
FFRDC	Federally Funded R&D Centre
GDP	Gross Domestic Product
ICT	Information and Communication Technology
IP	Internet Protocol
IPO	Initial Public Offering
IT	Information Technology
LEs	Large Enterprises
MNE	Multinational enterprise
NASDAQ	National Association of Securities Dealers Automated Quotation System
NIS	National Innovation System
R&D	Research and Development
RTO	Research and Technology Organisations
SMEs	Small and Medium-sized Enterprises
TBF	Technology Based Firm
p.a.	per annum

EXECUTIVE SUMMARY

Competitiveness: the key to success

Competitiveness of firms is crucial for their success in the market. Competitiveness of countries is crucial for their performance in terms of wealth creation. This report is about the competitiveness of the EU. The report is divided into two parts. Chapters 1, 2 and 3 present a general assessment of Europe's competitive performance, the main problems encountered and some of the explanatory factors behind these problems. The second part focuses on the strengths and weaknesses of the European manufacturing sector and compares its sectoral specialisation with that of the USA and of Japan. The first part of the report is directed towards the general reader. The second part analyses trends in sectors and industries and their underlying forces.

The problem: lag in wealth and employment creation

Europe lags behind both the USA (33%) and Japan (13%) in its standard of living, as measured by GDP per capita in purchasing power parities of 1997. In the past decade GDP growth averaged 2.5% p.a. in both Europe and the USA. In Europe this was primarily achieved by a combination of high growth of labour productivity with low growth of employment. The USA had low productivity growth and high employment growth.

In Europe *labour productivity* (GDP per person employed) is still nearly one fifth lower than in the USA, although Europe has been progressively catching up on the USA (see Fig. 1).

The substitution of capital for labour explains almost half of Europe's increase in labour productivity. For the USA this substitution effect is of limited relevance (see Fig. 2).

The speed of capital labour substitution depends importantly on the change in the relative price of labour (wages compared to the user cost of capital). There is evidence that the relative price of labour rose faster in Europe than in the USA.

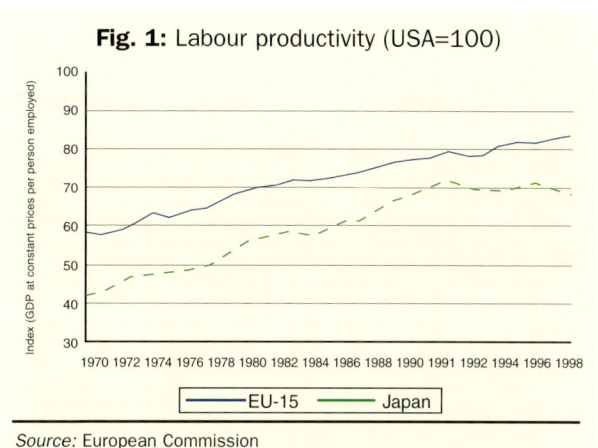

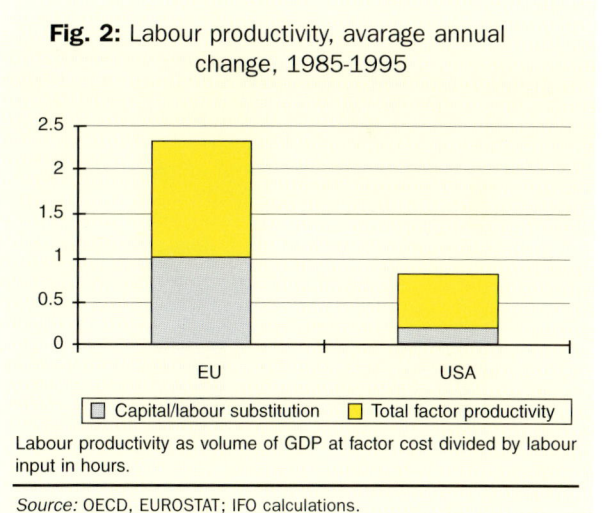

Fig. 1: Labour productivity (USA=100)

Source: European Commission

Fig. 2: Labour productivity, avarage annual change, 1985-1995

Labour productivity as volume of GDP at factor cost divided by labour input in hours.

Source: OECD, EUROSTAT; IFO calculations.

Europe's inability to create new jobs is resulting in a widening gap in employment rates (ratio between the total number of persons employed and the inhabitants of working age) compared to the USA and Japan (see Fig. 3). This is one of the main reasons behind the lower standard of living in Europe compared to the USA.

Europe's low job creation capability has several explanations. An important one is Europe's inability to move quickly into new, promising sectors. Where the USA has created jobs in technically advanced industries and transformed itself into a *service economy*, Europe is lagging behind (see Fig. 4).

EXECUTIVE SUMMARY

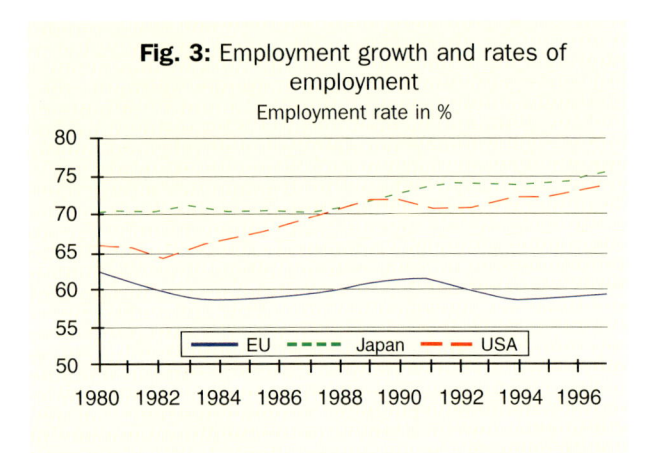

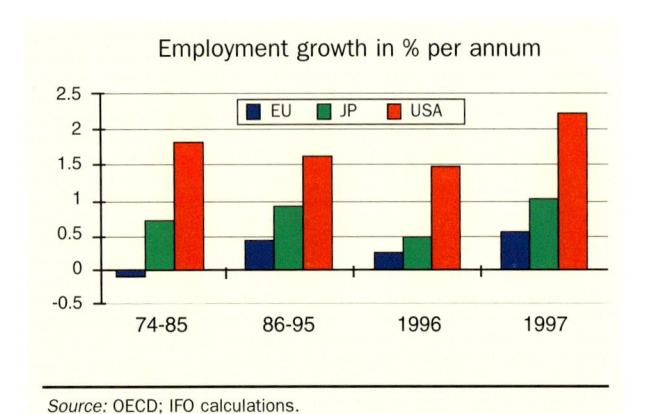

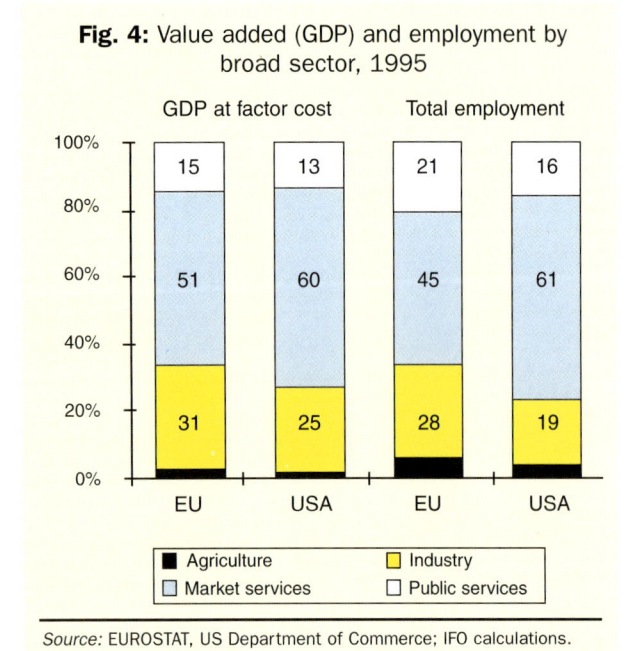

Fig. 3: Employment growth and rates of employment

Source: OECD; IFO calculations.

Fig. 4: Value added (GDP) and employment by broad sector, 1995

Source: EUROSTAT, US Department of Commerce; IFO calculations.

However, Europe's employment performance was weaker in all sectors between 1985 and 1995. This suggests that Europe's problems lie in the general environment for doing business rather than in the weak performance of individual branches of the economy.

Higher costs of basic services and labour

The *costs of basic services*, such as energy, transportation and communication are of great importance in staying competitive. Despite the Single Market Programme and its positive effects on competition and liberalisation, Europe still has more restrictions and distortions of competition in these service industries than the USA. The negative effect of these inadequate institutional conditions is illustrated by the higher prices which industrial users have to pay (see Fig. 5).

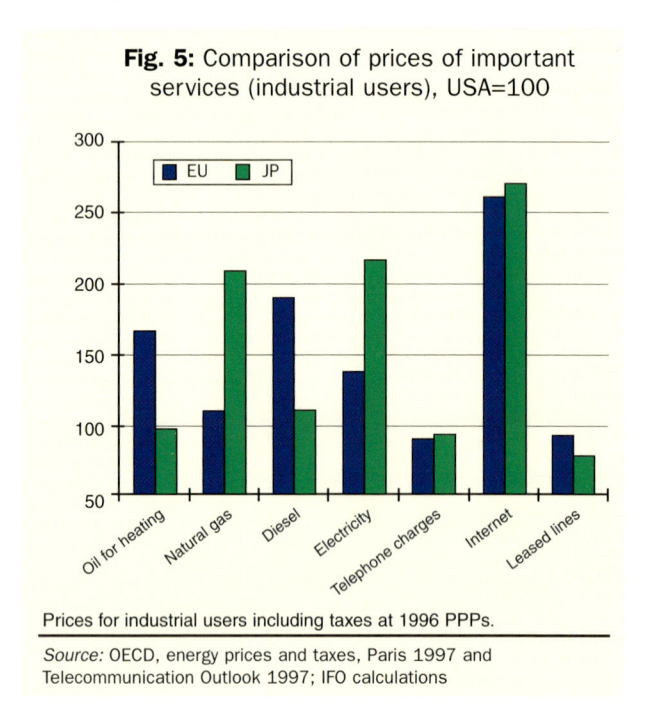

Fig. 5: Comparison of prices of important services (industrial users), USA=100

Prices for industrial users including taxes at 1996 PPPs.

Source: OECD, energy prices and taxes, Paris 1997 and Telecommunication Outlook 1997; IFO calculations

Wages and average nominal *labour costs* rose faster in Europe than in the USA during the 1980s, before increasing more or less in parallel during the 1990s. The greater increase in labour productivity only went some way towards mitigating the rise in labour costs so that unit labour costs still increased faster than those of the USA during this period (see Fig. 6). Measured in domestic currency, the relationship between nominal unit labour cost in Europe and the USA only stabilised after 1993.

Poor performance of innovation systems

Improving the performance of *national innovation systems* is also important for competitiveness. Commercially relevant innovation can be measured in different ways including the expenditure by business on R&D and international patenting. On both of these measures, Europe is lagging behind the USA and Japan (see Fig. 7).

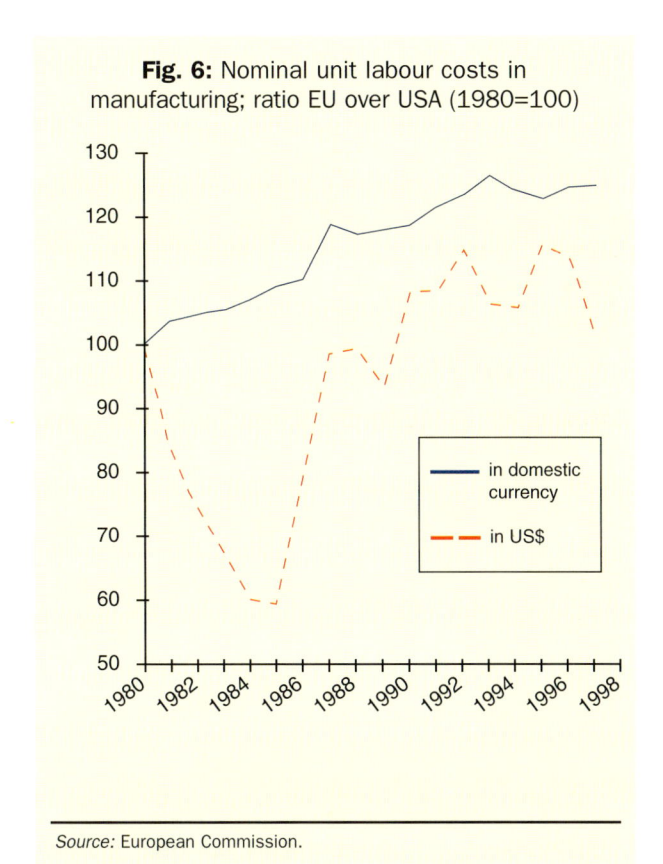

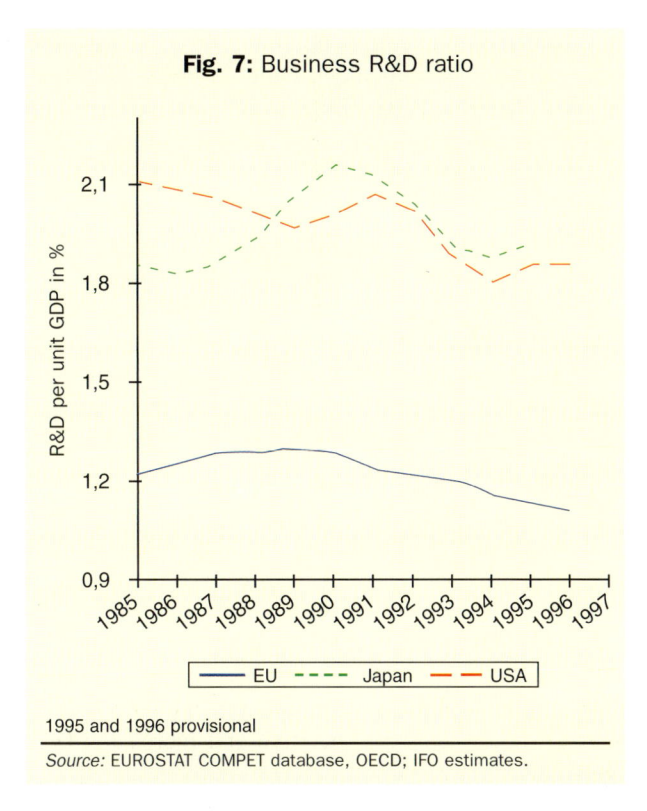

Fig. 6: Nominal unit labour costs in manufacturing; ratio EU over USA (1980=100)

Source: European Commission.

Fig. 7: Business R&D ratio

1995 and 1996 provisional

Source: EUROSTAT COMPET database, OECD; IFO estimates.

Relatively little patenting is undertaken by *public institutions*. Since in Europe, particularly amongst southern Member States, there is greater reliance on publicly funded R&D than in the USA and Japan, this constitutes a cause for concern. Explanations can be found in a number of areas. In certain countries, the inventor and not the public institution to which a researcher is attached holds the patent (Austria, Denmark, Germany and Sweden). This diminishes the incentive for such institutions to develop commercially relevant technology.

In Europe, compared with the USA, commercially relevant research is concentrated in non-university research institutions with the corollary of a greater separation between pure and applied research. This is significant because public institutions tend to concentrate on those fields of commercially relevant technology for which fundamental research is most important, especially biological and genetic technology (see Table 1). The breakdown by industry sector of public R&D institutions reflects this fact. The most important sectors are chemicals and pharmaceuticals, medical, optical and control and measurement instruments.

Table 1: Allocation of R&D output (EU, USA, Japan altogether) by field of technology

Cross-section technology	Inventions[a] in % filed by Universities	Research institutions	Industry
Information and Communication	16.3	34.3	76.8
Biological & Genetic Technology	79.1	55.0	11.7
Environmental Technology	4.6	10.7	11.5
All fields	100	100	100

[a] With origin in EU, USA or Japan, applied for patent in at least two countries between 1991 and 1996.

Source: EPIDOS, IFO Patent Statistics.

Lack of adequate risk capital

Most jobs are created by a small minority of high growth firms, often technology oriented. In the USA, 3% of firms accounted for 80% of job growth between 1991 and 1995. The competitive position of these firms is partly determined by the availability of a wide range of efficiently priced financial services. SMEs face problems in their access to financial resources. Compared to large enterprises they are restricted in their access to capital markets and institutions. Being very dependent on financial debt their relationships to banks are of particular importance. In addition, in specific areas particularly relevant for high growth firms, the framework for *financing SMEs* is less well developed than in the USA. This is especially true for business start-ups and the expansion of companies having entered new business activities. As a result, Europe has been slower than the USA in moving into the services

EXECUTIVE SUMMARY

market, especially business services, information, communication and media.

One of the reasons why Europe lags in high growth business start-ups is the *lack of adequate risk capital*. Compared to the USA, the European venture capital market is less likely to channel funds into companies involved in the seeding (research and development) stage or in the start-up stage. In 1997 this group of firms accounted for 29% of new investments in the USA while in Europe this was only 15% (see Fig. 8).

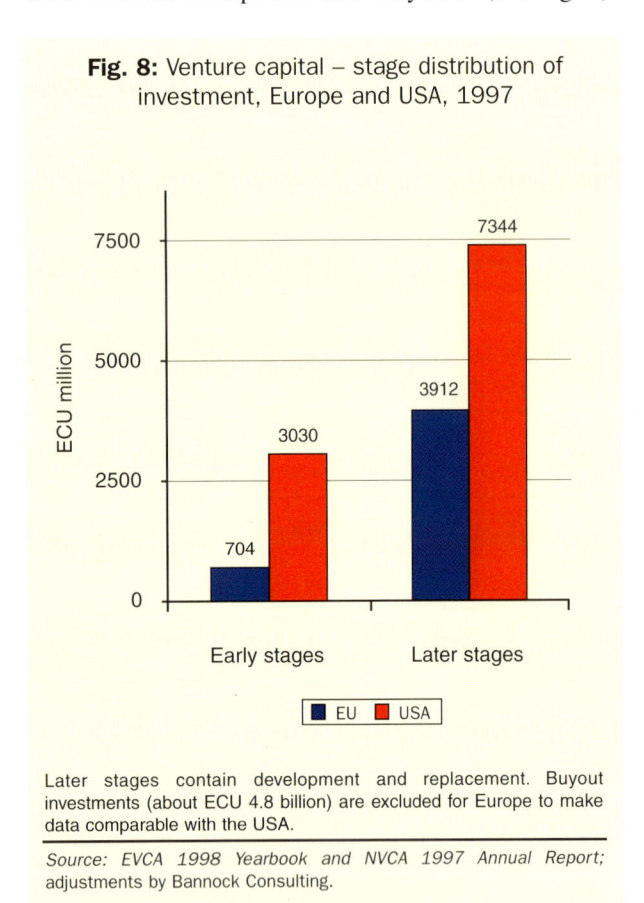

Fig. 8: Venture capital – stage distribution of investment, Europe and USA, 1997

	EU	USA
Early stages	704	3030
Later stages	3912	7344

(ECU million)

Later stages contain development and replacement. Buyout investments (about ECU 4.8 billion) are excluded for Europe to make data comparable with the USA.

Source: EVCA 1998 Yearbook and NVCA 1997 Annual Report; adjustments by Bannock Consulting.

Furthermore, venture capital in Europe is less associated with new technology-based firms compared to the USA. These firms are responsible for much of the development of the semiconductor, minicomputer, software and biotechnology industries. This is a key deficit in funding start-up and promoting rapid technological and sectoral change.

Behind the relative inadequacy of risk capital finance for high growth firms lies a lack of development of both demand and supply for risk capital. In order to diversify risk adequately, a large number of suitable projects in which to invest needs to be available. At the same time large, liquid markets with high degree of transparency and standards of disclosure are also required to encourage investors to participate.

Competitive strengths and weaknesses of European manufacturing

The purpose of the second part of the report is to identify strengths and weaknesses in competitive performance by looking at the current patterns and changes in the structure of the European manufacturing.

Following a similar pattern to that set for the economy as a whole, European manufacturing matched, between 1989 and 1996, both the USA and Japan in terms of nominal growth in value added, but performed worse in terms of employment.

With the share of the manufacturing sector in total GDP amounting to 20.6%, the EU is positioned between Japan (24.7%) and the USA (18.0%).

Overall performance of manufacturing industry

The overall performance of the manufacturing industry can be summarised as follows.

Given the lags of European manufacturing in terms of aggregate labour productivity, modest growth performance and rapidly declining employment, the sectoral analysis indicates neither overspecialisation in low productivity industries nor a lack of technological competence and manufacturing skills.

Compared to the USA, structural differences arise primarily from *poor performance in creating lead-time in the fast moving markets,* where competitive advantage is based on intangible investment in research and marketing. Since first mover advantages create substantial benefits in terms of growth and employment, the USA seems to have a greater ability to benefit from the particularly high growth dynamics in these industries.

External balances are not a constraint

Global competition: As a natural consequence of faster growth in other areas, notably in the dynamic Asian countries, the combined market share of the EU, Japan and the USA has declined. However, their overall trade balance is positive and increasing (see Table 2).

This implies that the global integration of world markets and the increasing competition with low wage economies may have reduced employment opportunities in specific industries, but not contributed directly to the overall decline in European manufacturing employment.

Table 2: EU manufacturing in a globalised world

	Share in value added (in%)		Value added growth (p.a., in%)	Share in world market (in%)		Trade balance (in ECU billion)	
	1989	1996	1989/96	1989	1996	1989	1996
EU	32.5	32.9	2.7	27.0	26.9	28.1	130.2
Japan	25.7	25.6	2.5	19.2	14.5	121.7	107.4
USA	41.9	41.6	2.4	20.2	18.8	-125.1	-146.4

Share in value added: EU+Japan+USA = 100. Share in the world market (market share): exports as a percentage of world imports.

Source: DEBA, COMPET; WIFO calculations.

Favourable external balances: External balances are currently not constraining European performance. The EU enjoys larger world market shares for its manufacturing exports than Japan or the USA. Despite increasing competition from emerging economies, the European market shares remained stable between 1989 and 1996. In contrast, both Japanese and US exports lost market shares in world imports. The EU's trade balance for manufacturing goods is positive and increasing.

European quality mark up: The European trade surplus is generated by a quality premium in the sense that exports are more highly valued than imports. This quality premium arises primarily from trade with countries other than Japan and the USA, e.g. in Central and Eastern Europe. As a consequence of Japanese specialisation in the export of goods from high unit value industries, the unit value of European imports from Japan is twice as large as that of exports to Japan. Comparing bilateral trade flows with the USA, the number of industries in which Europe has higher or lower export unit values is roughly equal.

Productivity

Gaps in labour productivity: Labour productivity of European manufacturing is significantly lower than that of Japan and the USA. The exact magnitude at the industry level is blurred by measurement problems, which stem in part from the interface between manufacturing and industry services. Differences in industrial structure do not affect the European productivity gap in manufacturing.

Modest catching up in productivity: Labour productivity in the EU is rising faster than in the USA. Given the large initial gap, catching up is progressing slowly. In past years, about one third of European productivity growth was due to structural change towards industries with higher productivity. This trend was supported by the simultaneous decline in employment shares in low productivity industries, e.g. in the clothing sector, as well as by growing shares of high productivity industries, such as pharmaceuticals. Although productivity growth is, for the most part, still affected by general factors that apply equally across industries, catching up relative to the USA would not have been possible without structural change.

Patterns of specialisation

Technological competence and skills: The EU proves its considerable technological competence and skills in mainstream manufacturing and the research-intensive industries outside the information technologies (see Table 3). The EU is most competitive in the sectors of machinery, vehicles and chemicals, which together create a trade surplus larger than the overall surplus of the EU.

Lags in fast moving, dynamic markets: European manufacturing compares poorly in the fastest moving markets, characterised either by recent technological upturns, as in the case of ICT-related research-intensive industries, or by rapidly changing consumer tastes. Compared to the USA, the low shares in total value added of research and advertising intensive industries reveal shortcomings in innovation and marketing strategies in these most dynamic markets.

Table 3: Competitive performance by type of industry

	Share in world market						Value added shares in the triad					
	EU		Japan		USA		EU		Japan		USA	
	1989	1996	1989	1996	1989	1996	1989	1996	1989	1996	1989	1996
	in %											
Labour intensive	28.0	25.6	11.5	9.4	10.4	9.8	35.0	35.4	28.3	28.1	36.7	36.5
Capital intensive	21.7	22.7	11.5	11.7	19.3	19.3	34.9	31.8	28.0	29.6	37.1	38.6
Advertising intensive	28.6	26.3	5.8	3.6	16.4	15.4	30.1	32.1	22.8	22.7	47.1	45.2
Research intensive	22.8	24.3	31.7	20.5	25.7	22.1	29.7	29.8	24.0	23.2	46.3	46.9
Mainstream manufacturing	40.0	37.4	23.1	17.6	21.3	21.0	34.0	34.1	27.6	27.6	38.3	38.4
Total manufacturing	27.0	26.9	19.2	14.5	20.2	18.8	32.5	32.9	25.7	25.6	41.9	41.6

Market share: Exports as a percentage of world imports.

Source: DEBA, COMEXT, COMPET; WIFO calculations.

European restructuring by multinational activity: European manufacturing is characterised by a significant increase in intra-EU multinational investment. This type of investment provides an important impetus for the ongoing restructuring of European manufacturing, especially in the industries relying largely on intangible firm-specific assets like innovation and marketing.

Required tailor-made policy

Four policy messages follow from the analysis of this report:

Elimination of institutional and regulatory barriers: Weaknesses were identified in some dynamic markets, characterised by product differentiation, marketing and innovation. The fast moving environment of these markets requires flexibility in entrepreneurial response. A prime policy target therefore is the elimination of institutional and regulatory barriers to the creative and flexible management of change. Such rigidities can be found in financial, labour and product markets, in particular in basic services, as well as in the highly disparate nature of European innovation systems.

Continuous upgrading of European industry: Unit labour costs in the EU are higher than in the USA, and - by a much wider margin - higher than in developing and transition countries. Low wage economies may successfully compete on price and may retain a presence in markets of homogenous and mature products. The EU needs to continuously invest in quality and to shift to new products at earlier stages of the product cycle. Economic policy in the EU has to promote, therefore, innovation, adaptability and the upgrading of human capital.

Sectoral analysis does not suggest any vertical targeting of individual industries by subsidies or strategic trade arrangements. In particular, two arguments support horizontal as opposed to vertical policies: (i) The policy of 'picking winners' generates opportunity costs relative to private market-based solutions. (ii) In addition, the analysis revealed that lower European labour productivity does not stem from structural weaknesses in the sense of being less specialised in high productivity industries than the USA.

Diffusion of best practice: A high degree of disparity within the EU was found to exist for example with regard to labour productivity. This underlines the importance of policies directed at the diffusion of best practices within the EU both in business and in policy.

Part One

The European economy

Chapter 1
Macroeconomic performance

An economy is competitive if its population can enjoy high standards of living and high rates of employment while maintaining a sustainable external position. Standards of living, measured by income per capita, remain on average in the 15-member EU well below those in the USA and in Japan.

The main factor behind this poor performance of the EU is the low growth of employment. EU Member States have succeeded over the years in raising their labour productivity at higher rates than in the USA. They have never matched, however, the record of the USA in employment creation. Compared to Japan, up until recently, they performed worse both in terms of productivity and of employment growth. Japanese productivity growth has lost pace in the nineties.

The poor employment creation record of the EU is related to a bias in favour of more capital intensive techniques and away from certain labour intensive sectors. Regulations and institutions in product, capital and labour markets are likely to have contributed to this bias.

1. Europe's competitive position

Gross domestic product (GDP) per capita is the main yardstick of living standards. In 1997, the GDP per capita in the EU still lagged well behind that of the USA and Japan. On average, a citizen of the EU enjoyed an income roughly one third lower than in the USA and one seventh lower than in Japan (see Fig. 1.1).

In terms of growth, throughout most of the seventies and eighties, European economies have done well relatively to the USA. Over that period, GDP per capita in West European countries converged to USA levels. Japan did even better. Starting in the sixties well below West European levels, its average income was in the early nineties some 10% higher than in the EU15 (excluding East Germany). Since the early nineties, however, GDP per capita in both the EU and Japan has regressed relatively to the USA (see Fig. 1.2).

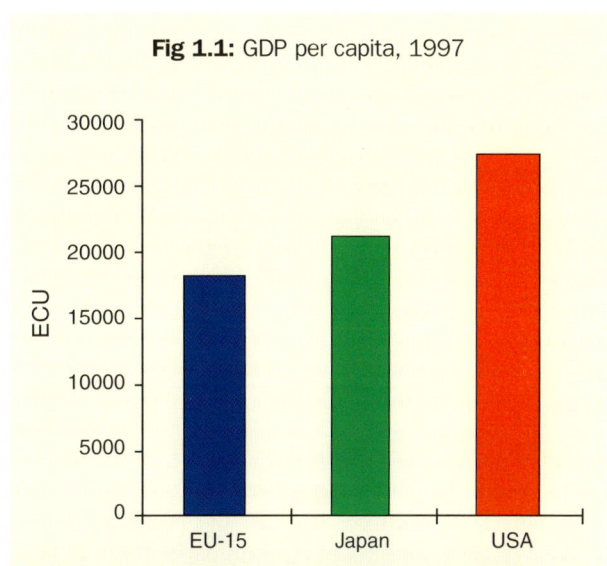

Fig 1.1: GDP per capita, 1997

In 1997 PPPs. Purchasing power parities (PPPs) are used for the comparison, because it is living standards that are analysed here. The level of real income in a country depends not only on the performance of the international sector of the economy, but also on the domestic sector.

Source: OECD; IFO calculations.

It may be argued that GDP per capita is the main but not the only indicator of a region's standard of living. The amount of leisure time, the level of social security and the degree to which the natural environment is protected also affect the welfare of the population. Environmental protection is also important in the context of the sustainability of GDP growth.

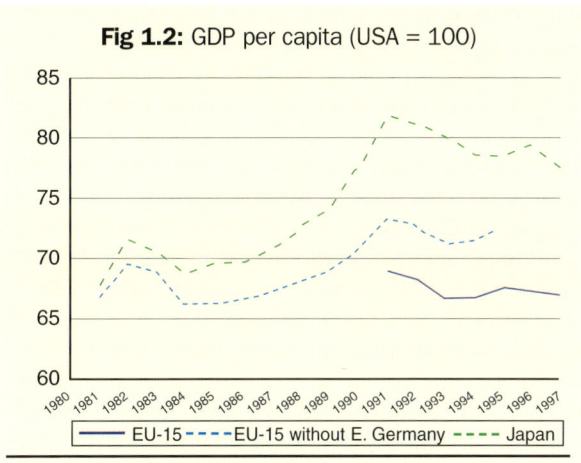

Fig 1.2: GDP per capita (USA = 100)

Source: OECD, German Statistical Office; IFO calculations.

Europe fares relatively better when some of these additional indicators are taken into consideration. For example, weekly working hours are shorter and employees have more holidays than in the USA and in Japan (see Table 1.1). Indeed, a significant part of the productivity increase in recent decades has been used to provide more leisure time to the employed population. At today's labour productivity, the extra leisure time in Europe compared to the USA is estimated to amount to 6% of total GDP.

Table 1.1: Leisure time

Standard 1996 for workers in manufacturing

Country/Region	Weekly Working hours	Number of days Holidays	Public holidays
EU 15	38.6	27.7	10.1
Japan	40	18	13
USA	40	12	11

EU 15 = Average of standards of Member States, employment weights.
Source: Institut der deutschen Wirtschaft, OECD; IFO calculations.

On the basis of some indicators, the EU also appears to be polluting the environment considerably less than the USA, both per head of the population (see Table 1.2) and in terms of emissions per unit of GDP (a measure of the environmental efficiency of production)[1]. Japan outperforms the EU in the area of SO_x and NO_x emissions. The environment efficiency of production depends both on industry structures and on the mix of energy sources and technologies used.

Table 1.2: Environmental pollution

Country/Region	Emissions 1995 per capita Tonnes of CO^2	Kg of SO_x	kg of NO_x
EU 15	8.9	31.3	32.7
Japan	9.2	7.2	11.1
USA	19.9	63.1	75.1

Source: OECD; IFO calculations.

These more positive aspects of the European economic system should not obscure, however, that at present a large part of the EU economy heavily under-utilises its capacity to produce and grow. A better macroeconomic performance would permit the European economies to pursue their social and environmental objectives more effectively.

---

[1] As a comprehensive set of indicators of environmental pollution for international comparisons is not yet available, the approach focuses on emissions which are of transnational importance and imply the danger of global warming and changes in climate.

2. Factors behind the lower European standard of living

The European gap in GDP per capita may be due to lower labour productivity per hour worked, shorter working time per employee, a lower employment-population ratio, or a smaller share of the population of working age (see Fig. 1.3).

Fig 1.3: Decomposition of GDP per capita

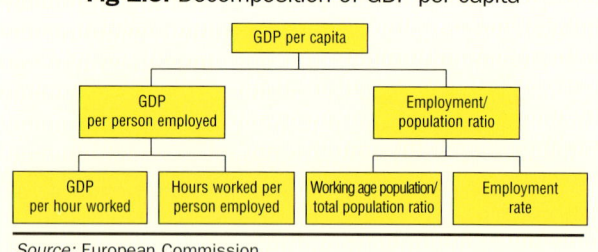

```
                    GDP per capita
                   /              \
          GDP                    Employment/
     per person employed        population ratio
         /        \                /        \
     GDP      Hours worked per  Working age population/  Employment
per hour worked  person employed  total population ratio    rate
```

Source: European Commission.

The extent to which these various components contributed to the lower level of European and Japanese GDP per capita compared to the USA is examined next in Figure 1.4.

Labour productivity relates to the business sector and is calculated as the ratio of GDP (at factor cost, constant prices) to the number of hours worked. For the calculation of hours worked, data is needed on the amount of part-time employment, the number of holidays and the daily working time. Internationally comparable data on these variables are currently only available up to 1995.

Fig 1.4: Factors explaining the gap in GDP per capita compared to the USA

Legend: Labour productivity (per hour); Working time (per person employed); Employment rate; Share of population at working age

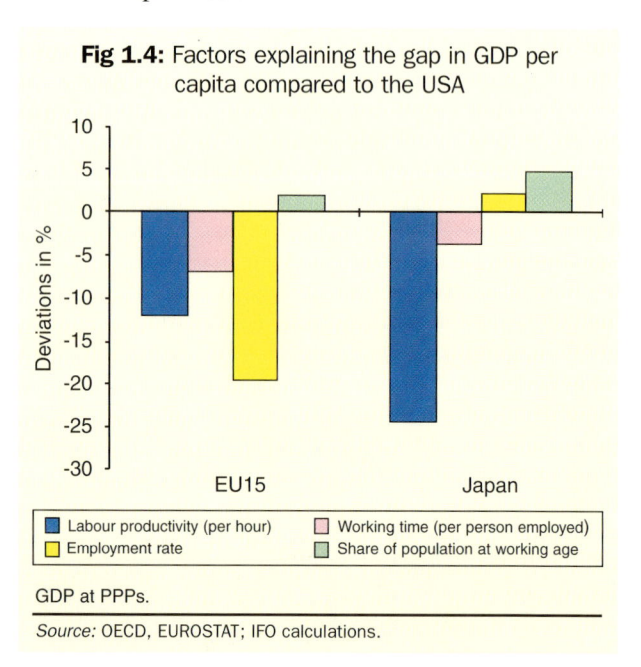

GDP at PPPs.
Source: OECD, EUROSTAT; IFO calculations.

The major factors explaining Europe's lower per capita GDP as compared to the USA are the lower employment rate and, to lesser extent, the lower labour productivity.

The employment rate is defined as the ratio of the total number of persons employed to the number of inhabitants of working age (15-64). Figure 1.4 also reveals that differences in working time between the EU and the USA play a less significant role than what one would have expected on the basis of Table 1.1. The larger proportion of part-time workers in the USA in part counterbalances the impact of shorter working time of full-time employees in Europe. Finally, it is worth noticing that the age composition of the population is currently in Europe's favour.

Japan has a labour productivity that is well below that of both the EU and the USA. The very low productivity in agriculture and services accounts for much of shortfall of the Japanese economy. On the other hand, it has an employment rate that is even higher than that of the USA. As a result, GDP per capita in Japan remains above that of the EU. Working time and the share of active population to the total population also work in Japan's favour.

The static Figure 1.4 does not tell the full story. Over the period 1985-1995 the contribution to GDP growth of rises in labour productivity and in labour input (total hours worked) has been rather different in the three areas considered (see Fig. 1.5).

Fig 1.5: Growth in labour input, productivity and GDP, 1985-1995 (% p.a.)

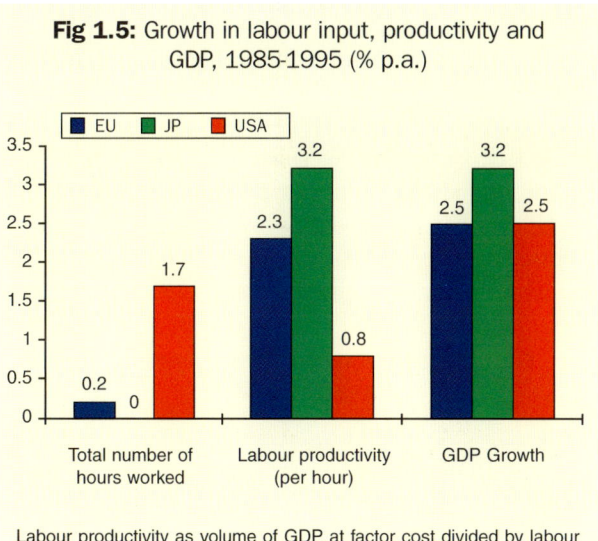

Labour productivity as volume of GDP at factor cost divided by labour input in hours.

Source: OECD, EUROSTAT; IFO calculations.

The European GDP growth of 2.5% p.a. was achieved by strong growth in labour productivity combined with low growth of the labour input. The rise of total hours worked has been close to zero. The same is true of Japan. Instead, the same GDP growth as in Europe was accompanied in the USA by a very significant rise of total labour input. Labour productivity in the USA has risen much slower.

3. Jobless growth: a constant feature of the European economy

In various degrees, 'jobless growth' has been a constant feature of the West European economies. It has recently appeared to be a characteristic also of the Japanese economy.

Over the last thirty years, labour productivity (GDP per person employed) in the current EU Member States has continued to rise faster than in the USA (see Fig. 1.6). Up until the early nineties, labour productivity in Japan rose even faster than in the EU.

Fig 1.6: Labour productivity (annual percentage growth)

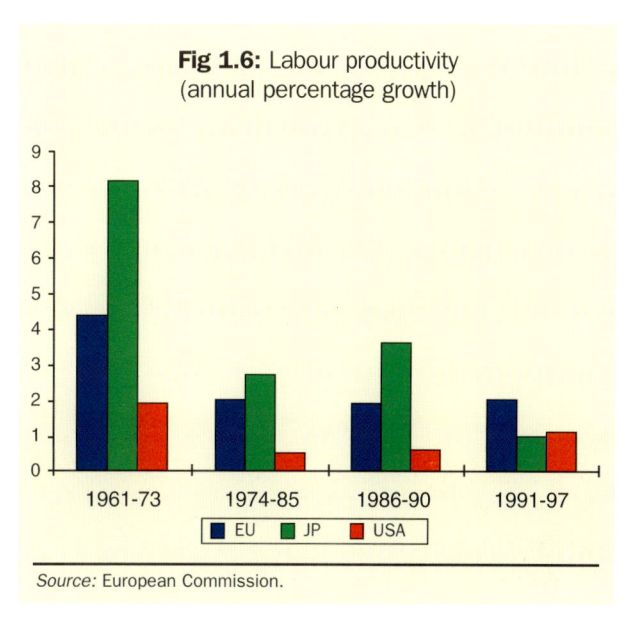

Source: European Commission.

The faster growth of productivity in the EU and Japan has allowed them to converge towards but not yet reach the US productivity levels (see Fig. 1.7).

Fig 1.7: Labour Productivity (USA=100)

Source: European Commission.

When turning to employment, the picture is radically different. The growth of numbers employed has constantly been lower in the EU than in the USA and in Japan. This was not only true in the turbulent phase of oil price shocks or during the fight against inflation in the seventies and early eighties. In the following decade of relatively high price stability, the European economy has continued to perform worse than either the American or the Japanese economy. Apart from fluctuations induced by the business cycle, the employment ratio in Europe has been stagnating at best. Compared to that of Japan and the USA, it has showed clear signs of divergence (see Fig. 1.8).

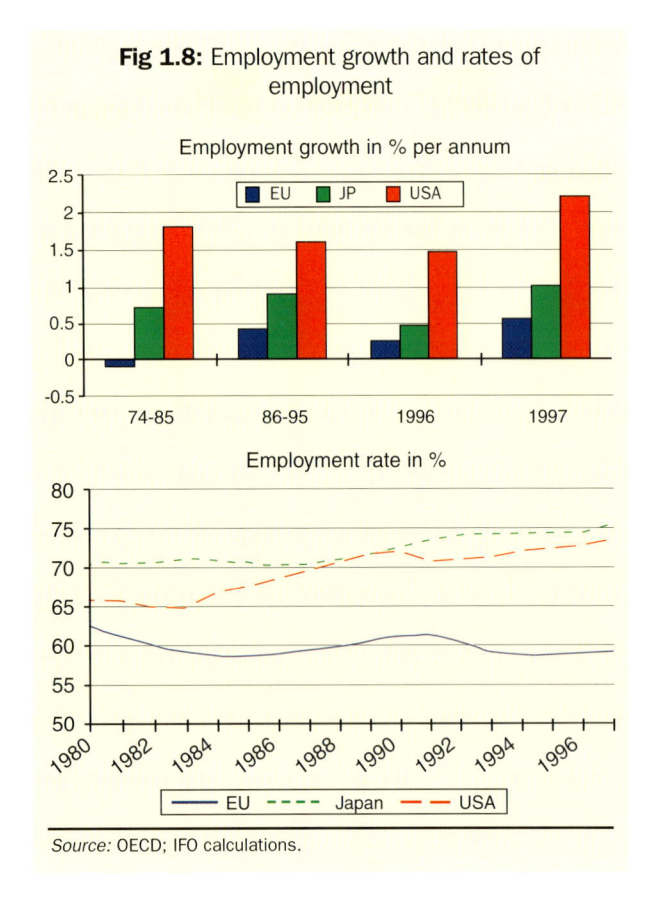

Fig 1.8: Employment growth and rates of employment

Source: OECD; IFO calculations.

Fig 1.9: Development in employment and labour input, 1985-1995 (% p.a.)

Source: OECD, EUROSTAT; IFO calculations.

Not only growth of numbers employed has been low in the EU but also, contrary to the recent USA experience, hours worked per person have fallen (see Fig. 1.9). In Japan the growth of employed people and the reduction of hours worked per person have cancelled each other out during the period 1985-1995. The net result has been no change in the total labour input.

There are two important aspects of the EU economy that help explain this jobless growth, at least in the more recent times. First, the EU has been relatively less specialised than the USA in services. Almost the entire net new job creation in the USA has been in this sector (see next section).

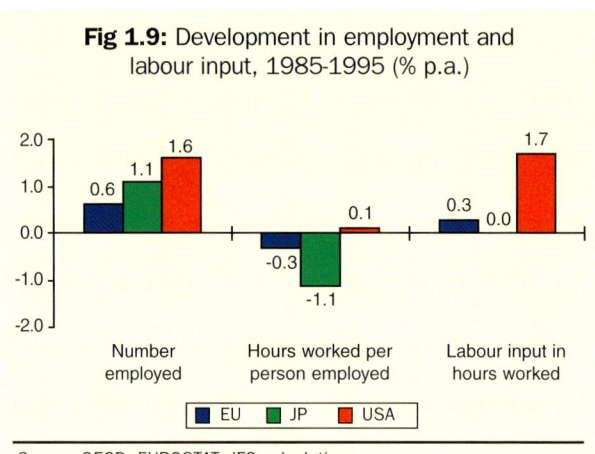

Second, productivity growth in the EU has tended to be accompanied by capital deepening much more than in the USA. Gains in labour productivity are the result of both total factor productivity growth and of capital/labour substitution. Growth of total factor productivity is the amount by which output increases as the result of improvements in methods of production, technology and organisation for a given amount of inputs. When an economy is in a state of full employment, capital/labour substitution permits faster growth than the underlying rate of increase in the labour force and technical progress would allow. If the same economy is functioning with spare employment capacity, however, capital-labour substitution may have undesirable job destroying effects.

In the EU, capital/labour substitution explains nearly half of the increase in labour productivity, whereas in the USA it has contributed only marginally to labour productivity growth (see Fig. 1.10). In Japan, it explains almost two thirds.

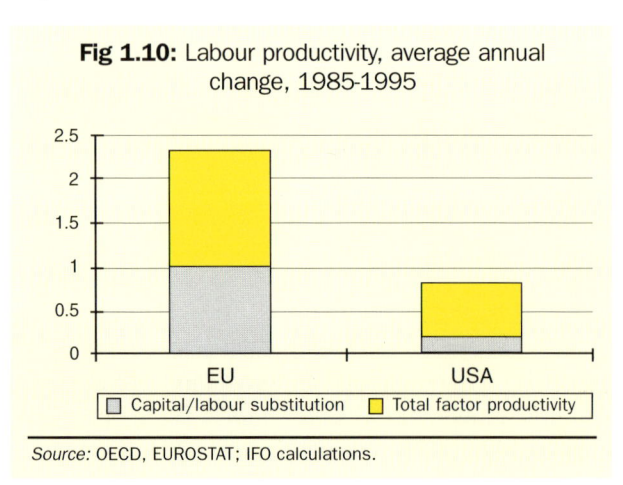

Fig 1.10: Labour productivity, average annual change, 1985-1995

Source: OECD, EUROSTAT; IFO calculations.

The speed of capital labour substitution depends importantly on the change in the relative price of labour (wages compared to the user cost of capital).

There is evidence that the relative price of labour rose faster in Europe than in the USA. Wages increased more than the prices of machinery and equipment (see Fig. 1.11). Real interest rates did not differ much between Europe and the USA in the last decade. The US tax reform in the second half of the eighties entailed disincentives for fixed capital formation.

Fig 1.11: Ratio of wages to prices of machinery and equipment

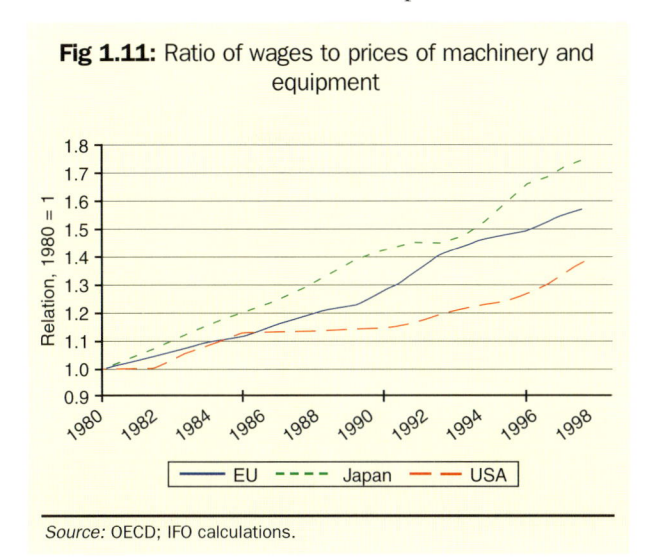

Source: OECD; IFO calculations.

4. Growth and employment in market services and manufacturing

The trend towards services has dominated the pattern of sectoral change for over two, three decades. Behind this trend is not only a higher income elasticity of the demand for services. Technical progress in the collection, storage, transmission and retrieval of information has reduced the costs of information and communication. Information services have become the centre of economic growth. These forces are fundamentally changing the organisation of production of goods and services and the way of life of society. Bearing in mind the importance of the trend towards services, the speed of adjustment of the sectoral structure of the European economy becomes an issue of competitiveness. The growth of productivity and of living standards is directly linked to the ability of the European economic and social system to encourage and manage this structural change.

A breakdown of production (value added at factor costs) and employment by broad sectors shows that the USA is a large step ahead on the way to the service society. The shares of both agriculture and industry in production and total employment are lower than in Europe (see Fig. 1.12).

Fig. 1.12: Value added (GDP) and employment by broad sector, 1995

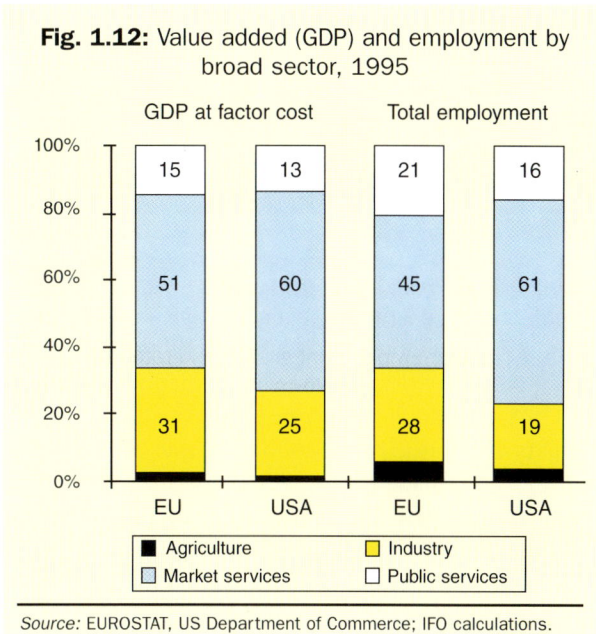

Source: EUROSTAT, US Department of Commerce; IFO calculations.

The difference in the share of industry also reflects different traditions in organising production. Industrial enterprises in Europe used to integrate service functions like catering, transport, accountancy and consultancy and have more recently discovered the advantages of outsourcing in this area. In the USA these services have been outsourced earlier and to a far greater extent to independent service companies.

As a late mover in the service-based economy, Europe is now in the process of catching up. Over the period 1985-1995, value added in market services has grown faster in Europe than in the USA. Employment in market services is, however, still growing more slowly in the EU compared to the USA (see Fig. 1.13).

Fig 1.13: Change of production and employment, 1985-1995 (% p.a.)

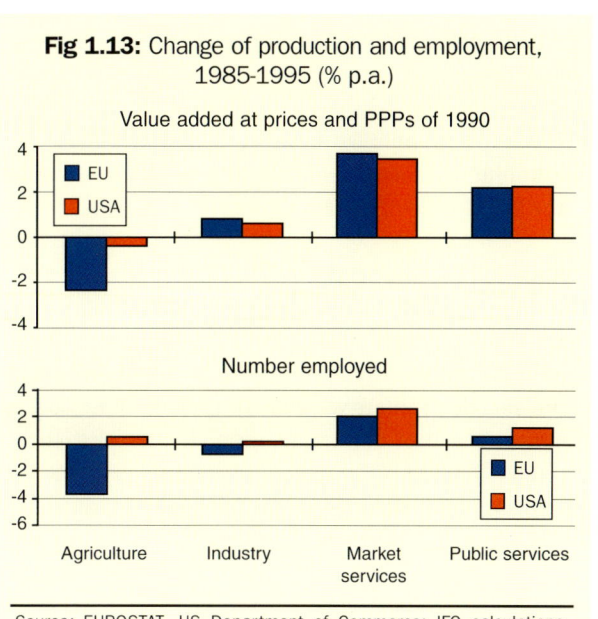

Source: EUROSTAT, US Department of Commerce; IFO calculations.

Though the developments in the service sector have clearly dominated employment growth in both the USA and the EU, the underlying problems of the EU economy are not limited to that sector. The USA economy has not lost jobs in any of the macro-sectors. In Europe, both agriculture and manufacturing have shed labour.

The pattern of development of the European manufacturing sector has been similar to that of the economy as a whole. Labour productivity rose faster but employment performance has been poorer than in the USA. As part 2 of this report shows, the European industry diminished its presence in low productivity sectors and increasingly concentrated on high productivity ones. This shift did not always have positive effects on employment. Instead, productivity growth in the USA did not depend on changes in the sectoral specialisation. Moreover, the European industry has trailed that of the USA in the development of some high growth research based sectors, such as ICT, that had positive spillovers to market services and, hence, to employment.

5. Costs of basic services and of labour

The adoption of more capital intensive techniques by European enterprises and their choice not to enter some of the more labour intensive sectors are both likely to be the result of the same underlying factors. In the product markets, especially those of services and public utilities, firms in Europe face important entry barriers. In the labour market, regulations and costs may induce firms to shy away from some labour intensive activities. In the capital market, a system biased towards stability of financial flows has tended to favour incumbents against new entrants and mature sectors against new areas of development.

The European innovation system and the role and functioning of capital markets are the subject matter of the two following chapters.

Prices of basic services

The total cost of business is determined to a significant extent by the prices paid for essential services like energy, transportation and to a decreasing extent communication. In the past these service industries were dominated by public enterprises and were subject to regulation restricting market access and the degree of international competition. This normally implies higher prices than under competitive conditions. In the USA these services were already liberalised in the late seventies or early eighties. Despite the Single Market Programme and its positive effects on competition and liberalisation, Europe still has more restrictions on and distortions of competition in these service industries. Privatisation has just begun. Delayed privatisation and liberalisation are reflected in the higher prices that industrial users have to pay (see Fig. 1.14).

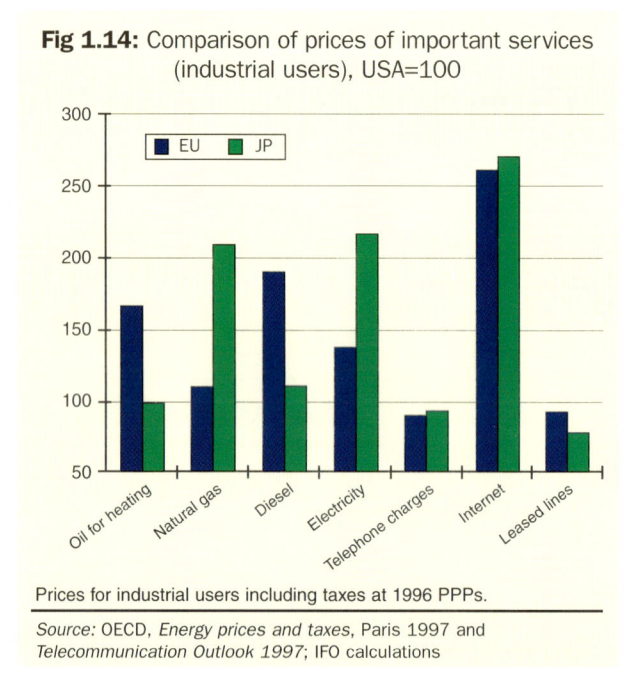

Fig 1.14: Comparison of prices of important services (industrial users), USA=100

Prices for industrial users including taxes at 1996 PPPs.

Source: OECD, *Energy prices and taxes*, Paris 1997 and *Telecommunication Outlook 1997*; IFO calculations

As a rule, the prices of the selected services are higher in the EU than in the USA. This is especially true of energy, whether for heating, processing or transportation. Electricity, the main energy source for automation and handling, is also more costly for business in Europe. Compared to Japan, only natural gas is cheaper in Europe.

In the case of heavy and light fuel oil and automotive diesel oil, the higher price levels in Europe also reflect significantly higher tax rates on energy for business use in Europe. Natural gas and electricity are no longer taxed in most EU countries.

It is interesting to note that the liberalisation of telecommunication services for European business, which resulted in considerable price cuts[2], brought telephone charges for business down to US levels as early as 1996. The price of leased lines has also declined to US levels. This price is not only important for data communication by large and medium-sized companies.

---

[2] Pending liberalisation also exercised pressure on prices in those countries where *de jure* a monopoly of the national public telecommunication operator (PTO) still exists. For details see OECD, *Telecommunication outlook* 1997, Paris 1997, pp. 99-101.

It also determines the market entry chances for resellers of telecommunication services. Only the cost of Internet access, which is also important for SMEs, is considerably higher in Europe. This mainly reflects the fact that in the USA the cost of local calls is determined on a flat rate basis as part of the basic service.

Within the EU, costs tend to rise from North to South, both for energy services and for telecommunication services. Only Ireland constitutes an exception to this pattern. The higher costs for business in Southern European countries often reflect greater delays in the liberalisation of service markets.

Compared to US industry, European business also has to cope with higher costs for other services. A McKinsey study[3], comparing productivity in Germany and France with US levels, showed European costs to be 10 to 20% higher in the provision of software services and construction services due to lower productivity.

Labour cost

In the case of industries subject to international competition, the development of unit labour costs in manufacturing industry may be used as an indicator of the cost position. Wages and average nominal labour costs rose faster in Europe than in the USA during the 1980s, before increasing more or less in parallel during the 1990s. The greater increase in labour productivity only went some way towards mitigating the rise in labour costs so that unit labour costs still increased faster than those of the USA during this period (see Fig. 1.15). Measured in domestic currency, the relationship between nominal unit labour cost in Europe and the USA only stabilised after 1993.

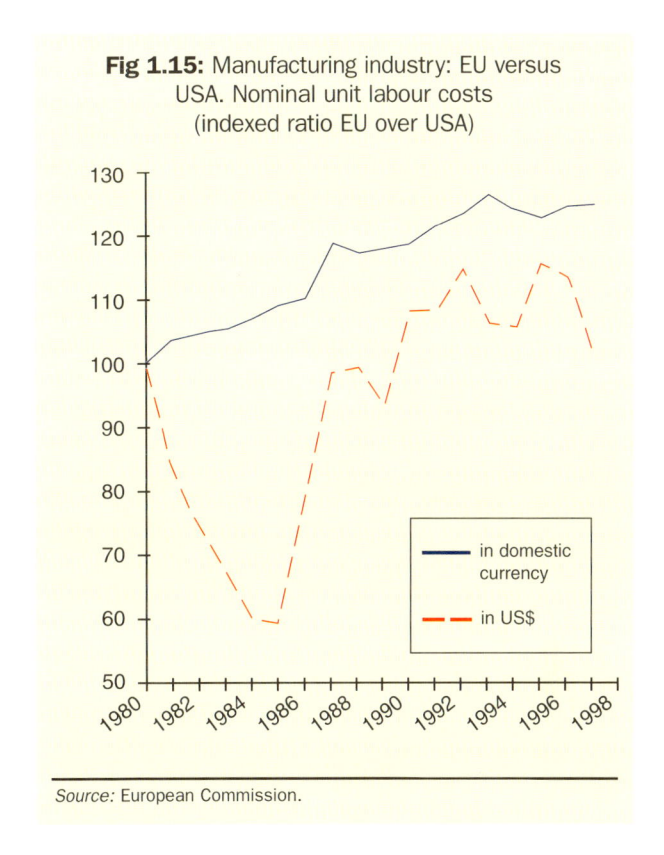

Fig 1.15: Manufacturing industry: EU versus USA. Nominal unit labour costs (indexed ratio EU over USA)

Source: European Commission.

Changes in nominal unit labour costs have been swamped by developments in exchange rates. In 1980, the dollar was at a historical low compared to the ECU, implying a favourable position in the cost competitiveness of US industry. Throughout the period 1987-1997 the ratio of unit labour costs measured in dollars was near or above that prevailing in 1980. The pressure to rationalise and to cut costs by restructuring and closing down unprofitable activities was high.

---

[3] McKinsey Global Institute: *Removing barriers to growth and employment in France and Germany,* Frankfurt, Paris, Washington, 1997.

Fig 2.2: Global patents by region of origin [a]

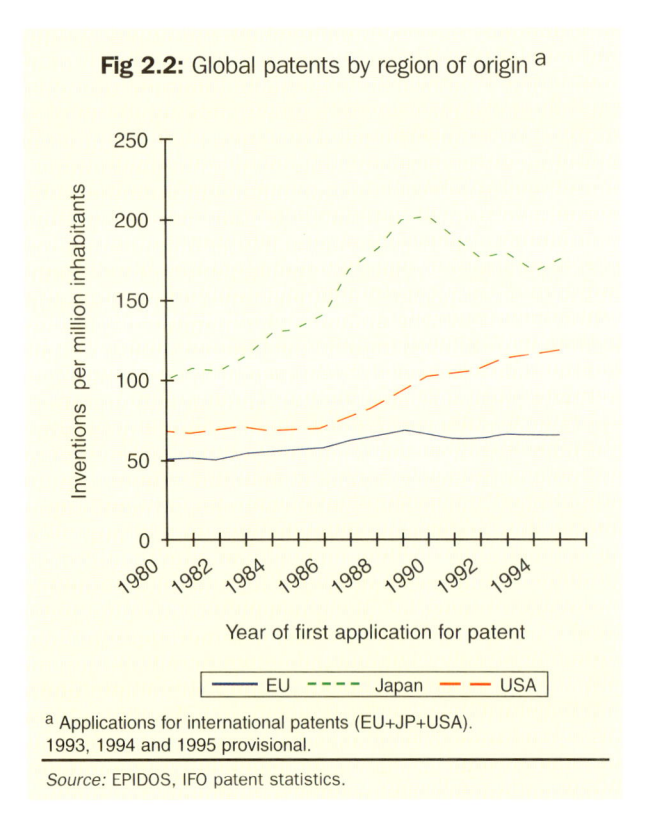

[Chart: Inventions per million inhabitants vs Year of first application for patent, 1980–1994. Lines for EU, Japan, USA.]

[a] Applications for international patents (EU+JP+USA). 1993, 1994 and 1995 provisional.

Source: EPIDOS, IFO patent statistics.

R&D output measured by this indicator shows that US inventions per capita were higher than those in Europe and continued to increase despite the decline in R&D expenditures relative to GDP. The decline in patenting by Japan after 1990 reflects financial difficulties experienced by Japanese companies since the early nineties, although Japanese invention activity has still remained at a higher level than in the USA.

In the EU, internationally relevant R&D output per capita stagnated during the nineties and there are scarce signs of an upturn. This mirrors the decline in R&D efforts of business. The gap vis-à-vis the USA is widening, although the American innovation motor has also lost some steam. Japan is undergoing an even more pronounced decline than Europe, but still has a higher level of R&D input and output than Europe.

Country specific differences in innovation activities can be explained by differences in national systems of innovation. The publicly funded R&D infrastructure plays a key role in these systems. The first part of this chapter looks at the similarities and differences in the organisation of the public scientific base between Europe, Japan and the USA, and its role in knowledge generation. Part 2 takes up the issue of the economically relevant R&D output of public research institutions and asks how the efficiency of public research institutions could be improved in terms of economically usable output.

National innovation systems are specialised. To achieve and maintain successful performance it is necessary to move into segments promising a rich potential for growth and job creation. Parts 3 and 4 of this chapter therefore discuss Europe's performance in information and communication technology and biotechnology. These are two areas with major growth potential and with pronounced effects on economic and social structures.

1. Role and types of national innovation systems

Current literature on innovation emphasises the importance of national systems of innovation in explaining differences in the volume of innovation and the different paths that innovation may take. The main actors in a national innovation system (NIS) are firms, public and private research organisations, and government and other public institutions. These actors are influenced by a variety of factors: the financial system and corporate governance, legal and regulatory frameworks, the level of education and skills, the degree of labour mobility, industrial relations and prevailing management practices[2]. Figure 2.3 shows the main components of and interconnections within NIS[3]. The efficiency of NIS generally depends on interactions and the interface between various actors and the working of the system as a whole. This section focuses on one particular part of the knowledge generation side of the total system: the public research infrastructure (the higher education sector, other publicly funded research bodies).

The institutional profiles vary between countries depending on the governance regime of enterprises, the organisation of the university sector and the level and orientation of government-funded research. In contrast to most European countries, the US university sector includes numerous research institutes (e.g. federally funded R&D centres, FFRDCs) carrying out the same type of R&D activities as specialised R&D research centres in Europe. Due to the weaker R&D performance of the business sector in southern European countries, the public research institutions must play a relatively large role in R&D. To improve the link between publicly funded knowledge production and private industry all countries have created special transfer institutions.

---

[2] Some of these factors are analysed in other chapters of this report.

[3] See OECD, *Technology, Productivity and Job Creation - Best Policy Practices,* Paris, 1998.

Fig 2.3: Elements of national innovation systems

Source: OECD.

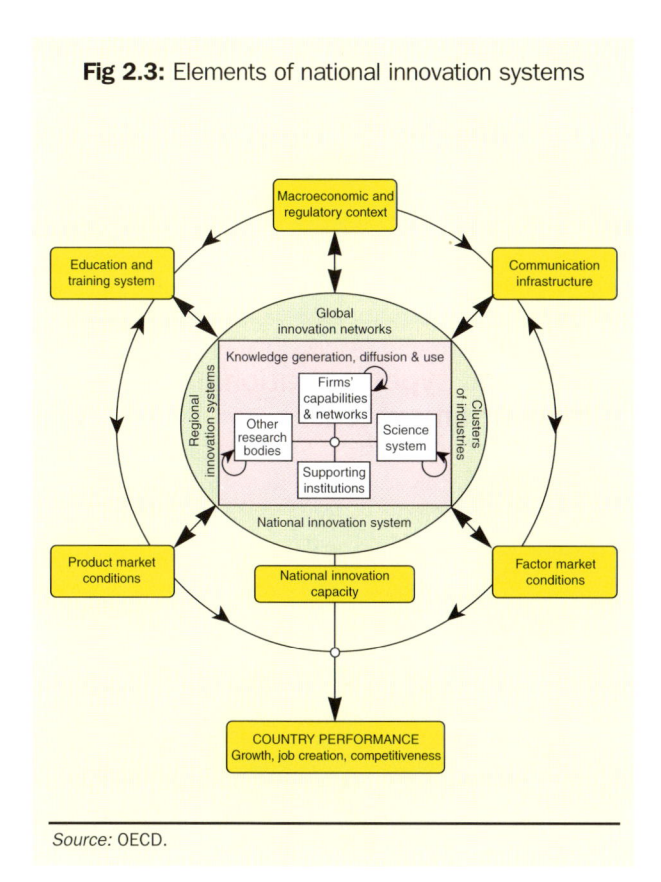

The public part of the innovation system consists of a variety of institutions (see Table 2.2). Universities and technical colleges represent in some sense the cornerstone of NISs, with responsibility for providing higher education and performing basic research. However, links to applications are growing, and the borderline between science and technology in frontier areas of research is becoming increasingly blurred.

Whereas in the USA 100 research universities out of a total of 3000 universities and colleges constitute the backbone of basic research, Europe relies more heavily on non-university research. There are large differences between universities, both nationally and internationally: the research activities and objectives of universities like Stanford or MIT, and the substantial applied R&D effort of US state universities, often far more closely resemble the big science institutions in Europe than the research profiles of European universities. Japan lacks a strong public infrastructure for basic research. The R&D systems of the larger EU countries (France, Germany, Italy and UK) cover, as in the USA and Japan, the full range of publicly funded research institutions. In the smaller EU countries, there are only few big research centres (partly financed by the EU) alongside the higher education sector. The main R&D efforts are located in Research and Technology Organisations (RTO).

The diversity of European systems has both strengths and weaknesses. On the one hand, it presents an opportunity to exploit the specialisation, complementarities and synergies of national research efforts. On the other hand, it involves the risk of aiming limited resources at too many national institutions with similar functions and objectives across the countries. A way of overcoming the disadvantages of fragmented national innovation systems has still to be developed.

Table 2.2: Public research institutions

Types	Examples
Institutions in the higher education sector	Universities, Technical Colleges
Big national science networks	National Centre for Scientific Research (E), Centre National de la Recherche Scientifique (F), National Research Centres (D)
Specialised government research establishments	Centre for Energy Research (NL), National Agency for New Technologies, Energy and Environment (I), Department of Energy Laboratories (USA)
Other non-university research institutions: • Research and technology organisations (RTO) • Institutions for applied research • Laboratories	Certified Research and Technology Organisations (DK), TNO (NL), Fraunhofer Society (D)

Source: IFO Institute.

In Europe, the amount of GDP spent on different R&D agents (higher education sector, non-university research institutions, and business sector) varies greatly between northern and southern countries. As the R&D/GDP ratio declines, the relative weight of publicly financed research institutions in terms of researchers and funds increases (see Fig. 2.4).

In most countries the business sector (industry) accounts for at least 50% of total expenditure, except in Spain, Greece and Portugal. Differences in business R&D explain the differentials within Europe. Greece, Austria, Portugal and Spain allocate more than 30% of their R&D expenditure to the higher education sector. The highest level of R&D expenditure in the non-university sector occurs in Greece, Portugal and France. France is the only country where R&D spending in the non-university sector is greater than expenditures for the higher education sector.

Fig 2.4: R&D expenditures in % of GDP by country and research institution

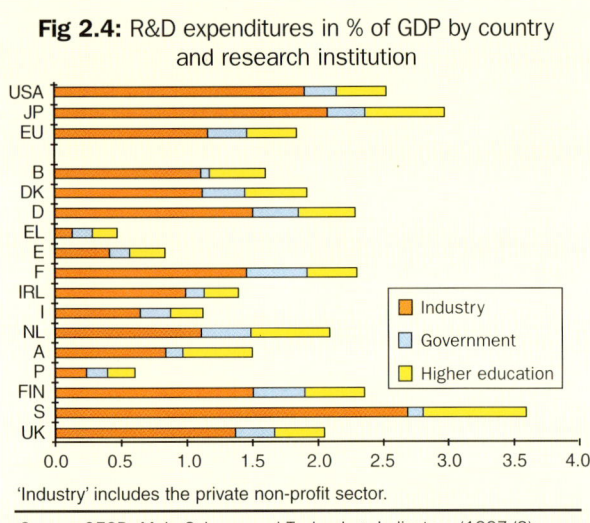

Source: OECD, Main Science and Technology Indicators (1997/2).

'Industry' includes the private non-profit sector.

The transfer of knowledge from the public research institutions (universities, big science institutes) to industry is especially difficult because of differences in orientation, researcher motivation, and institutional culture. That is why many countries established specific bridging institutions to link public R&D establishments more closely to industry. In the Netherlands a number of intermediary organisations like the Dutch Innovation Centres and the Regional Development Agencies assist in the transfer of knowledge generated in the public infrastructure to the private sector. The UK technology transfer system consists of various intermediaries, including institutions which are directly or indirectly associated with the flow of technology and transfers like the Business Support Organisations. Although there are more than 1000 bridging institutions in Germany, an evaluation of this system showed that the most successful way to bring together R&D generators and R&D users is still direct contact between researchers of R&D institutions and industry[4]. The USA have had a similar experience. Technology transfer may be initiated *ex ante* by funding joint research projects or *ex post* by helping with the exploitation of existing knowledge.

2. Efficiency of public research institutions

In the era of globalisation, national innovation systems may have lost some of their importance. New and cheaper information and communication technologies and improved regulation of intellectual property rights have facilitated and improved both the transparency of technological developments and international technology access and transfer. On the other hand, there are studies showing that the home base provided by public R&D institutions is still very important for innovation, especially for small and medium-sized enterprises. Furthermore, budget constraints are forcing governments in many industrialised countries to increase accountability as well as effectiveness and efficiency of government supported research.

Measuring the efficiency of public research institutions is a difficult task (see Box 2.1). Taking patent activity as the yardstick, the share of public R&D institutions in total patent activity is low in all regions covered (see Table 2.3).

Table 2.3: Importance of public institutions for economic relevant R&D output

Country/region	Universities	Non-university research institutions	Total public
EU	0.7	2.1	2.8
USA	3.5	1.5	5.0
Japan	0.1	0.2	0.3

Share in % of all inventions [a] filed for patent 1991-1996 by

[a] Patents applied for in at least two countries with origin in USA, EU or Japan

Source: EPIDOS, IFO Patent Statistics.

Corresponding to the bigger role of research universities in the USA and non-university research institutions in Europe, the contribution to patentable R&D output of US universities is higher than that of European universities.

Within Europe, there are considerable differences between countries in the number of inventions per researcher (see Fig. 2.5). The differences do not, however, mirror differences in the 'productivity' of public institutions concerning economically relevant R&D output. Rather, they reflect, on the one hand, national differences in the 'patent regimes' for universities and other public research institutions. In some countries patents can only be owned by individual researchers, in others by the universities, in still others by the state. On the other hand, the impact of special organisations for the exploitation of R&D results can be observed.

---

[4] M. Reinhard, H. Schmalholz, *Technologietransfer in Deutschland: Stand und Reformbedarf,* Berlin-München, Duncker & Humblot, 1996.

Box 2.1: Possibilities of and limits to measuring R&D output of R&D institutions

As there is no simple measure of the volume and quality of R&D institutions' output, proxy indicators have been developed. They rely on:
- Bibliometric data (publication counts; citation analysis; co-citation analysis; co-ordination and bibliographic coupling);
- Peer review and other systems;
- Measures of esteem (invited papers at international conferences; short-term migration; secondment or visiting researchers; honours or professional status indicators).

These approaches have proven useful for the evaluation of the scientific performance of researchers and institutions, but are less applicable to measuring economically relevant R&D output. For this purpose other indicators are used:
- Patent data (patent counts; patent citation analysis),
- Number of spin-off companies,
- Innovation counts,
- Innovation surveys.

Patent counting is a well-established approach for measuring economically relevant R&D output. Output is measured by counting R&D results which have passed (or are expected to pass) the screening of patent offices for technical novelty and degree of innovativeness. This measurement approach guarantees a minimum quality standard. It cannot, however, cover innovations, which do not enjoy intellectual property protection under patent laws (e.g. software, purely organisational changes). For the analysis here all patent applications worldwide were taken into account (about half a million inventions for which patents were applied in at least two countries between 1991 and 1996).

To measure the patentable R&D output of public institutions the applications from universities and research institutions were identified and aggregated by country of origin. Information from several handbooks or from reports on national innovation systems was used to decide on the status (private or public) of individual research centres and laboratories.

A major problem of this approach is that the number of patents of public R&D institutions does not necessarily cover all their economically relevant R&D output, as patent filings which arise as a result of a privately funded project of a public R&D institution are generally registered and paid for by the industrial partner. In addition, due to country-specific regulation of intellectual property rights, the ability of public research institutions to file for patents may be constrained. The performance of R&D institutions may also be affected by their science base, because patent affinity differs by fields of science. Statistical analysis shows that rates of patenting are high in certain research areas, such as pharmaceutical research. But scientific fields with lower rates of patenting, such as engineering, need not necessarily have a lower technology transfer potential. This is why this has to be taken into account when comparing R&D institutions across fields of technology. This also applies to country ranking, as countries specialise in different fields of technology.

The relatively low patent/researcher ratio in Austria, Denmark, Germany and Sweden is due to the fact that in these countries intellectual property generally belongs to the inventor (if he is a faculty member of the university). Consequently, by law the universities have few possibilities of developing their own patent and licensing programmes. The situation is different for British universities which, because of their legal structure, can almost be managed as economic entities. A specific utilisation organisation, the British Technology Group, holds patents on behalf of universities and generates an income of approximately £ 15 million p.a. purely from licenses for university research, which implies a high value of the knowledge produced. Such industrially relevant knowledge is concentrated in particular fields, such as pharmaceuticals, metallurgy, and engineering. But this should not obscure the fact that where returns are identifiable, they seem to be high.

In France, a similar situation can be seen. At the beginning of the 1990s a specific utilisation organisation was established, called *France Innovation Scientifique et Transfer* (FIST). In Germany a pilot project is still running to improve the patent assisted marketing of university inventions.

Fig 2.5: Patentable inventions per researcher in public R&D institutions
- Inventions[a] per 1000 researchers -

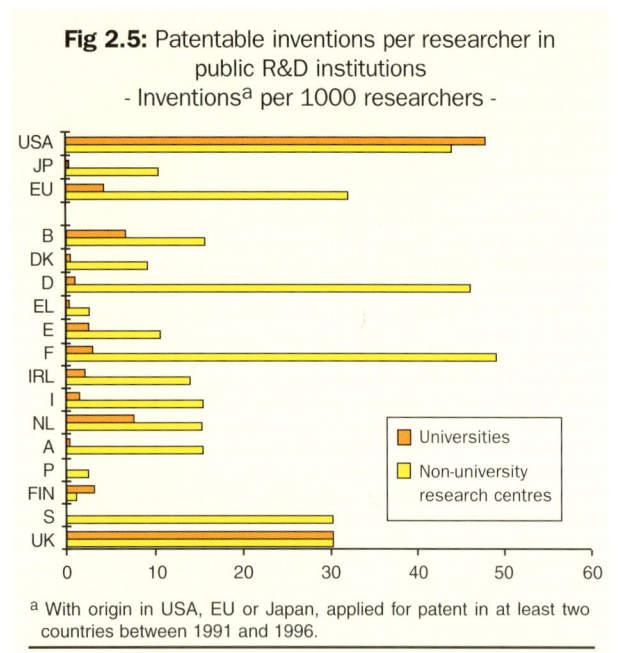

[a] With origin in USA, EU or Japan, applied for patent in at least two countries between 1991 and 1996.

Source: OECD, Main Science and Technology Indicators (1997/2), EPIDOS, IFO Patent Statistics.

In general, publicly funded R&D establishments play a subordinate role for R&D output of economic relevance. But they can be spearheads for the development of new technological paradigms. This is also indicated by the allocation of R&D output of public R&D institutions by today's major cross-section technologies (see Table 2.4). Publicly funded research institutions, especially universities, focus on biological and genetic technology whereas industry concentrates on ICT innovations. This is also true if the EU, the USA and Japan are considered separately. US

Table 2.4: Allocation of R&D output (EU, USA, Japan altogether) by field of technology

Cross-section technology	Inventions[a] in % filed by		
	Universities	Research institutions	Industry
Information and Communication	16.3	34.3	76.8
Biological and Genetic Technology	79.1	55.0	11.7
Environmental Technology	4.6	10.7	11.5
All fields	100	100	100

[a] With origin in EU, USA or Japan, applied for patent in at least two countries between 1991 and 1996.

Source: EPIDOS, IFO Patent Statistics.

universities have the strongest focus on biotechnology. This corresponds to the state of development of the science base. In the young biosciences, the commercial exploitation of scientific breakthroughs has just begun. In information and communication technology, the basic scientific breakthroughs already occurred in part in the first half of the 20th century. This technology has now reached the stage of general application and improvements to detail have come to dominate. As a result, it has become principally the domain of industry and of less interest to scientific institutes. Technologies for environmental protection, where application of 'old' knowledge from different scientific branches to new problems prevails, are also unattractive for public R&D institutions.

As non-university research institutions are often closer to application of scientific knowledge than universities, it is no surprise that their patentable R&D output has an allocation that is closer to industry (see Table 2.4). The allocation of inventions of public R&D institutions by field of technology relevant to certain industries also differs considerably from the allocation of inventions by private business (see Fig. 2.6). The pronounced concentration of public research institutions on technologies relevant to chemistry mirrors the orientation of their patentable R&D output on biotechnology. This technology is especially important for pharmaceuticals. The commitment of public R&D to health issues is reflected in the disproportionately high share of inventions relevant to the manufacture of medical, optical, and control and measurement instruments.

Fig 2.6: Allocation of R&D output of private enterprises and public institutions by industry
- Distribution of inventions[a] in % -

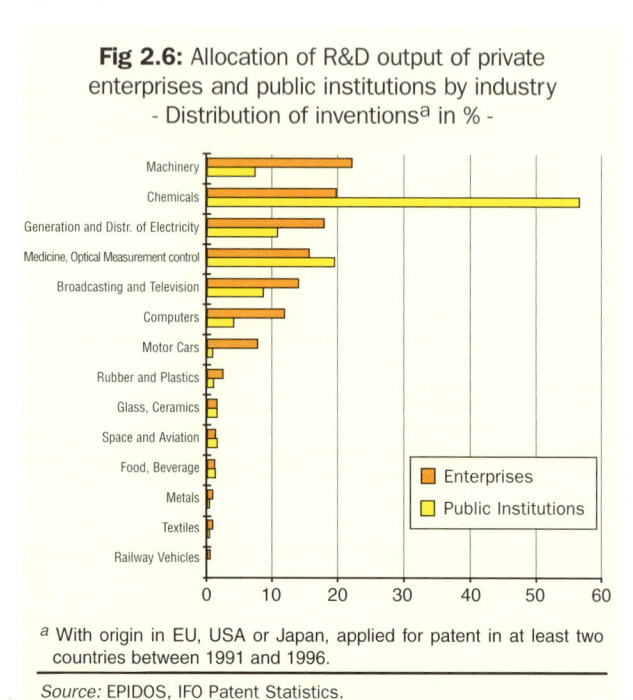

[a] With origin in EU, USA or Japan, applied for patent in at least two countries between 1991 and 1996.

Source: EPIDOS, IFO Patent Statistics.

A closer look at the allocation of R&D output of public institutions by industry in Europe and in the USA reveals interesting differences. The well-known European diversity and R&D programmes for special industries has led to a greater diversity in R&D output of public institutions in Europe (see Fig. 2.7).

Fig 2.7: Industrial focus of public R&D institutions in EU and USA[a]

[Bar chart comparing USA and EU across: Chemicals, Medicine/optical instr., Food/beverage, Glass/ceramics, Air and space, Electricity G.+D., Communication/TV, Textiles, Metals, Rubber/plastics, Computers, Machinery, Motor Cars, Railway vehicles; scale 0–300]

[a] Ratio of the number of public inventions to business inventions

Source: EPIDOS, IFO Patent Statistics.

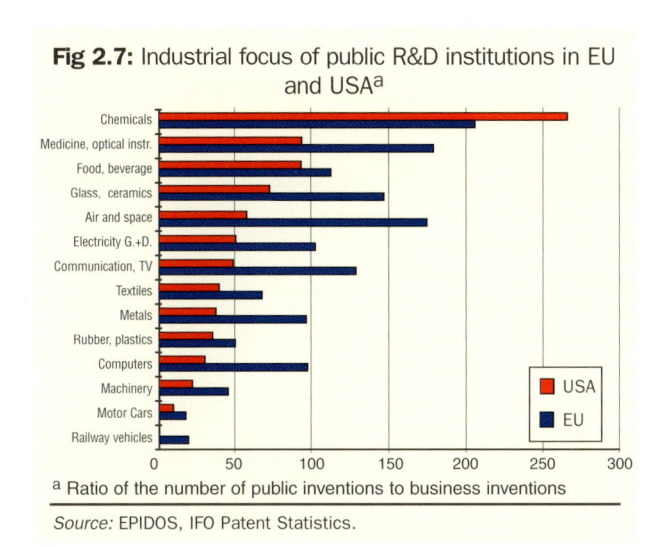

In order to show differences in emphasis, Figure 2.7 compares the ratio of the number of inventions of public R&D institutions to business inventions by industry with the corresponding ratio for all inventions in the different regions. The approach controls both for differences in the size of technology fields (industries) and differences in the propensity to patent of public R&D performers. Values above 100 indicate a special focus of public institutions in the region on this field of technology, relative to industry.

A common feature of public institutions in Europe and in the USA is their R&D output has greater importance for the stream of inventions in chemicals, and medical and optical instruments. Another common characteristic concerns the fact that they contribute little to the technological advance in machinery, motor cars and railway vehicles. US public R&D output is, however, far more focused on the 'domain' of patentable public R&D output, e.g. chemicals. Perhaps associated with European programmes promoting R&D in aerospace, information technologies and 'new materials', European public R&D institutions focus more than US institutions on new solutions in the aerospace industry, in the production of communication equipment and TVs and in the glass and ceramics industry.

The last paragraph showed that national innovation systems specialise in different areas of technology. The specialisation is grounded on their specific knowledge base. To achieve and maintain a successful country performance it is necessary to move into segments with high growth potential. How did the innovation systems perform in Europe, Japan and the USA with regard to the two key technologies leading into the next decade: information and communication technology and biotechnology?

3. Information and communication technology

Information and communication technology (ICT) is viewed as a pervasive technology with a major impact on business and society. Its diffusion is expected to generate a new paradigm in the organisation of production and work (decentralising, home-working, customising), new and/or cheaper distribution channels and a bundle of new or better information-based services. The diffusion of digital information and communication technologies has entered a new phase[5]. Digital processing, communication, storage and retrieval of all kinds of information (images, sound, voice, text and data) has become possible without the need for any transformation between the different states of information. New networking technologies and software produce a significant expansion of communication capacity. Increased capacity and the deregulation of the communication markets result in big reductions of communication costs The digitalisation of communication is the key to knitting together the isles of automation of the past. It is the missing link for the electronic integration of the spheres of business and private households and for unleashing the full potential of ICT for the improvement of productivity in industry and services. Because of its pervasiveness and its potentially revolutionary effects on productivity, production and demand structures, it will change patterns of living, lifestyles of people and political systems around the world. The technology is viewed as the driving force of the transition to the post-industrial era and therefore as essential for competitiveness.

Both in terms of demand and production, ICT has been growing rapidly in recent years. ICT markets are subject to growing globalisation, and growth in ICT demand has also picked up in Europe. Prime movers include the Internet, the development of electronic commerce, and especially, the liberalisation of telecommunication services. Many national and supra-national campaigns to make users aware of the major

---

[5] The diffusion of ICT already started in the fifties with the use of mainframe computers in business and of TV sets in private households. The seventies saw the entry of computing in the factories (industrial robots, automated transport systems) and in distributive services (automated storage system). The triumph of the personal computer (PC) in the eighties made the automation of office work possible and laid the foundations for new services for consumer and business. Mobile phones considerably improved the accessibility and voice communication for individuals. The nineties are seeing the digitalisation of communication of images, sound, voice, text and data.

cultural change help to develop and expand markets. The European ICT industry is still quite a way behind their American and Japanese counterparts. Europe has, however, a relatively strong position in the production of telecommunication equipment and also in measuring, checking and controlling equipment. American suppliers dominate the software market for standardised office applications.

In 1997 the worldwide ICT market had an estimated volume of ECU 1225 billion. Taking hardware and software together, the size of the computer or IT based market equals the communication market (see Fig. 2.8). The hardware market for computers, office equipment and data communication hardware is three times greater than the market for telecommunication equipment. But the market for telecommunication services is larger than the combined markets for computer services (support, operations management, consulting and implementation) and software products (package software and especially designed software).

The market directly affected by the diffusion of ICT technologies is even larger and comprises, in addition, audio-visual equipment and media services (films, TV and music production, and publishing houses). Together with the software services, the latter form the so-called copyright industries because their business is crucially dependent on copyright regulations. The competitive framework of these industries will be fundamentally changed by the rise of electronic commerce via the Internet. At more than ECU 150 billion, the world market for audio-visual equipment is larger than the market for telecommunication equipment but smaller than the market for computer hardware. Due to definition problems and severe gaps in the statistical coverage of production and international trade,[6] the size of the markets for media services cannot be determined even roughly.

In ICT industries goods and services are becoming increasingly closely related. Developed countries are moving towards an information society with new solutions and needs in many activities and corresponding market segmentation (entertainment, training and education, electronic commerce, communication). ICT markets are also subject to growing globalisation, as companies seek the most cost-effective structures, trade barriers remain relatively low, and demand for ICT products and services is of a universal nature. Both in terms of demand and production, ICT in the more narrow definition has been growing at a fast pace in the last few years (see Fig. 2.9).

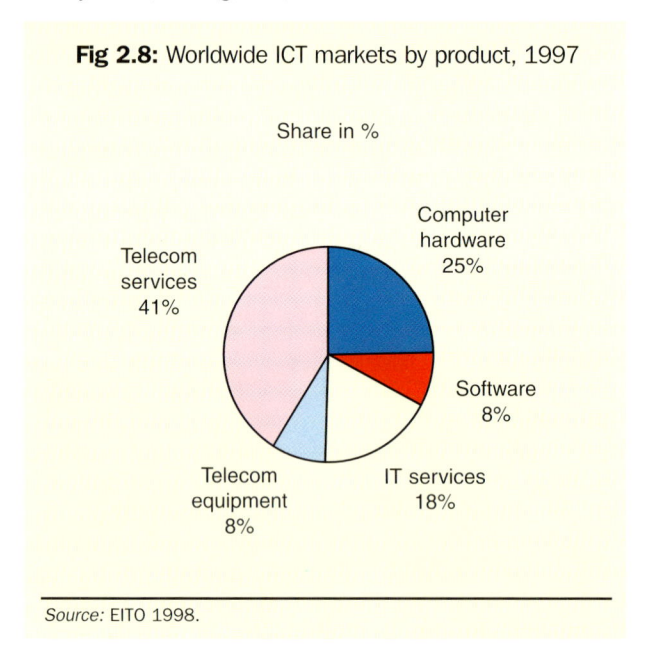

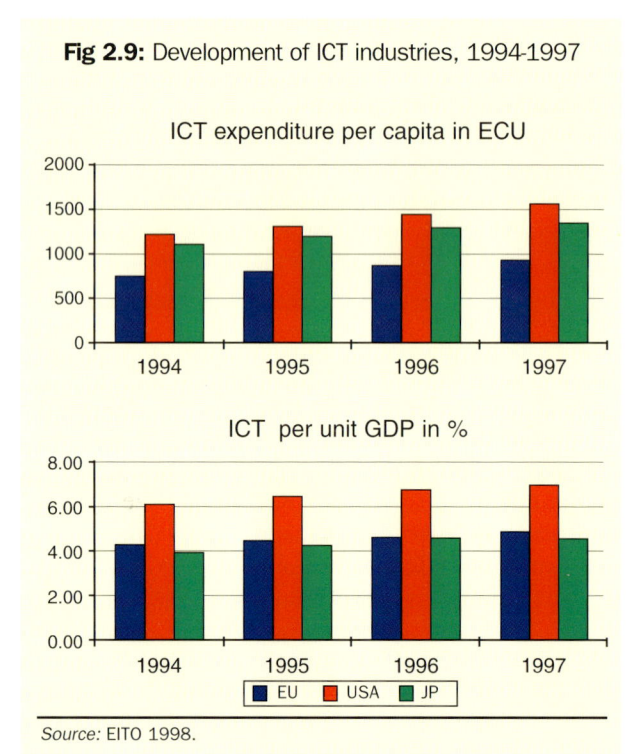

Fig 2.8: Worldwide ICT markets by product, 1997

Share in %
- Computer hardware 25%
- Telecom services 41%
- Software 8%
- IT services 18%
- Telecom equipment 8%

Source: EITO 1998.

Fig 2.9: Development of ICT industries, 1994-1997

ICT expenditure per capita in ECU (1994-1997)

ICT per unit GDP in % (1994-1997)

EU ■ USA ■ JP

Source: EITO 1998.

The superior growth performance of the American ICT industries reflects a successful restructuring in response to the challenges posed by the diffusion of PCs, client-server networks within firms (partly substituting for mainframe computing) and the Internet (creating a potential for new IT services). In the USA the restructuring of ICT industries started at the beginning of the 1990s (e.g. IBM and Digital Equipment Corporation). Restructuring was

---

[6] For details see OECD, *Working party on the Information Economy: Measuring electronic commerce: International trade in software*, DSTI/ICCP(98)3/Final, Paris, 1998, p.7 ff.

accompanied by massive job losses in the USA and the elimination of 'old champions' from the market. But at the same time, dynamic new companies gained important positions (Microsoft, Compaq, Sun, Cisco etc.). ICT now ranks as the top industry in the USA. ICT accounted for 6.1% of GDP in 1996 against 5.4% in 1990, most of this additional growth being in services (software).

With 4.3 million jobs ICT firms are the single largest manufacturing employers, with about 10% of the manufacturing workforce. After a net job decline between 1990 and 1994, nearly half a million jobs were created by these industries in 1995 and 1996, pushing up demand for highly skilled workers and, accordingly, their salaries. In the USA, the emergence of new service companies and restructuring made the industry stronger, eventually leading to better employment prospects.

The same restructuring phenomenon is now apparent in Europe. The impact of these measures is sometimes taken as a sign of declining competitiveness, whereas in fact it is part of a process that might eventually strengthen the whole industry and provide a base for new job creation. European industry still trails its American or Japanese counterparts. As with employment, the shares of the European ICT firms in total EU, US and Japanese output remain below the corresponding manufacturing industry averages (see Table 2.5).

Table 2.5: European position in ICT

	Production 1996	Share of total production of EU, USA, Japan (%)		
Nace	Manufacturers of	EU	USA	JP
3210	Electronic components	9.7	41.6	48.7
3000	Office equip., computer	23.4	39.2	37.4
3220	Telecommunication eq.	33.6	28.2	38.3
3230	Audio and video	25.1	7.3	67.6
3325	Measuring, control eq.	34.2	46.8	19.0
	Electronic industries	22.8	34.8	42.3
	Total manufacturing	39.2	33.8	27.0
	3325= 3320 + 3230			

Source: DEBA; IFO calculations.

There are pronounced differences within the electronics industry. Europe has a relatively strong position in the production of telecommunication equipment and of measuring, checking and controlling equipment. The latter is the heart of automation in processing and assembling industries. During the 1990s, European industry has already improved its position in semiconductors and telecommunication equipment and has maintained its position in consumer electronics. The Japanese software industry is now in a less favourable position than its European counterpart.

After being depressed by the European recession of 1992/93, ICT demand growth picked up again (see Fig. 2.10). General business conditions for the near future are favourable in Europe, in particular with the prospect of increasing economic convergence. ICT-specific growth factors include the adoption of the Internet Protocol (IP) and of new Internet facilities, the development of electronic commerce, the liberalisation of telecommunication services, national and supra-national campaigns to make users aware of the cultural change, and last but not least, the introduction of the Euro and the problem of the Millennium bug.

Thus in Europe, ICT market prospects are good: according to EITO, in the period 1997-1999 overall ICT spending is expected to grow at annual rates of around 8%. Trends are significantly different for the telecommunications and information technology (IT) sectors. The growing use of telecommunication networks (the volume measured in terms of time or quantity of information transported) will be partially balanced by declining tariffs. IT market growth in value terms is expected to remain buoyant, as demand for software and IT services is gaining strength.

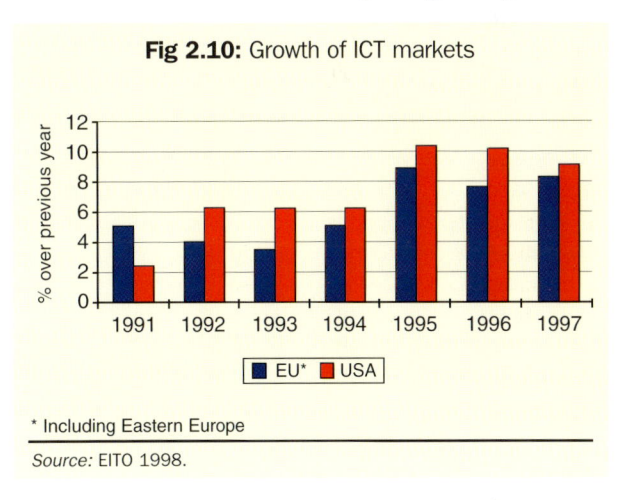

Fig 2.10: Growth of ICT markets

*Including Eastern Europe
Source: EITO 1998.

European markets lag behind those of other regions because:

i) EU companies often regarded ICT as a cost element and not as a key factor in improving competitiveness, streamlining business or promoting innovation.
ii) Compared to the USA or Japan, the take-up of ICT by individual EU consumers is slow, with the exception of the Nordic countries and some other bigger countries (see Table 2.6).

iii) The fact that telecommunication liberalisation is taking place in Europe at an uneven pace acts as a brake on growth. The success of the GSM standard shows the importance of promoting an adequate regulatory framework.

The rapid ICT diffusion in Nordic countries reflects tax incentives to boost demand: incentives have been offered to employees in Sweden, Denmark and the Netherlands for the acquisition of modern personal computers, sometimes with exceptional success.[7]

ICT industrial structures in Europe have been slow to adjust to new challenges, speedy adjustment having been the key to success in the USA. Outsourcing, developing networks of competitive component suppliers and cross-national production networks are the strategies that paid off on vast ICT global markets. The dynamic growth of new entrants into the market (particularly SMEs) has also been better in the USA than in Europe.

Table 2.6: Possession of modern ICT equipment

Country/ region	Up-to-date PCs[a]	Internet hosts	Mobile phones	Cable TV
USA	259	31	165	239
Japan	141	4	143	26
EU 15	113	7	84	95
UK	145	10	116	29
Germany	149	7	67	217
France	105	3	43	39
Italy	59	2	112	0
Spain	52	2	76	48
Finland	157	59	292	161
Sweden	227	22	282	200
Denmark	223	15	265	187
Netherlands	177	14	66	382
Austria	130	10	75	108
Ireland	54	6	74	145
BLEU	103	5	50	357
Portugal	45	2	67	11
Greece	27	1	49	0

Per 1000 inhabitants in 1996

[a] Stock of PCs acquired between 1994 and 1996.

Source: EITO 1998, OECD; IFO calculations.

Finally, EU industries have difficulties competing on price because of the high level of labour costs. Seeking excellence in quality could be a solution, as has recently been done in GSM mobile telephones and digital satellite TV. Development of adequate software is a key factor for the future because the role of software in conferring competitiveness and providing added value in ICT industries is extremely important.

4. Biotechnology: Europe keeps pace

Biotechnology is 'the application of scientific and engineering principles to the processing of materials by biological agents' (OECD). Biotechnology is a young and promising sector with great potential for improving Europe's standard of living (through reduced pollution, better use of natural resources and improved healthcare) and also for raising productivity in a wide range of industries: healthcare, agriculture, food and drink, chemicals and environment. Together, these industries represent about 9% of the EU's gross value added and 8% of its employment.

The industry has reached a more mature stage in the USA than in Europe (see Table 2.7), but Europe's performance has been improving recently. Thus, the number of specialised biotech companies in Europe has increased from 580 in 1995 to 700 in 1996. According to the European Association of Bioindustries, the value of products and services using biotechnology in Europe could reach 250 billion and affect more than 3 million jobs by 2005, against ECU 40 billion[8] and 300-400 000 jobs in 1995.

Table 2.7: Key biotechnology indicators

Indicator	Europe	USA
Turnover (ECU million)	1 700	11 700
R&D expenditures (ECU million)	1 500	6 300
Number of companies	700	1 300
Publicly quoted companies	50	300
Number of employees	27 500	118 000

Source: Ernst & Young 1997.

Biotechnology remains close to basic science. This is not only because biotech companies are often located near universities with strong bioscience departments or adequate scientific research centres. It is also reflected in the relatively high share of universities, public research institutes, foundations and government organisations contributing to patentable product innovation in the EU and the USA: 23% and 38% of patentable inventions, respectively, originated in such institutions between 1990 and 1995.

---

[7] For example, the Wall Street Journal of 18 March 1998 reports that following a tax cut offered to the members of a Swedish trade union (LOO) for modern equipment to improve their skills, Hewlett-Packard's Swedish desktop PC sales were more than four times higher in the fourth quarter of 1997 than they were in the corresponding period of 1996.

[8] Human Healthcare: ECU 8 billion; Agriculture: ECU 5 billion; Food and Drink: ECU 17 billion; Environment: ECU 1 billion (total: ECU 40 billion).

As the industry directly transforms scientific progress into processes and products, the success of companies crucially depends on their R&D results and on their ownership of industrial property rights. Taking into account the size and stage of development of the US market, the American industry has the largest share of R&D output for which a patent is sought, but Europe ranks second, well ahead of Japan (see Fig. 2.11). Success stories in Europe include the Danish company *Novo Nordisk* which holds the record for biotechnology patents in the 1990s.

A survey of companies by the European Association of Bioindustries[9] shows that the three most important external factors which influence investment decisions are the scale of market opportunity, the effectiveness of patent protection and the regulatory framework (pressure from competitors having the same ranking as the latter). A positive attitude toward entrepreneurship is a key to success in this sector. The survey pointed in particular to the availability of equity capital, regulations on the use of biotechnology, intellectual property protection, fiscal policies and the provision of adequate skills. In general, there seems to be greater awareness of the growth potential of biotechnology in the USA than in Europe.

countries more, in particular the USA. The analysis of the European innovation system and of the efficiency of the public research institutions shows a great potential for creating new technologies. In order to promote growth and create knowledge intensive jobs it would be necessary to mobilise this potential by changing or improving the regulatory framework in some European countries.

Fig 2.11: Biotechnology invention activity

Inventions for which international patent applications have been made (EU, USA, JP) by country of origin

USA — Japan — Other — EU-15 — World

1993, 1994 and 1995 provisional.

Source: EPIDOS, IFO Patent Statistics.

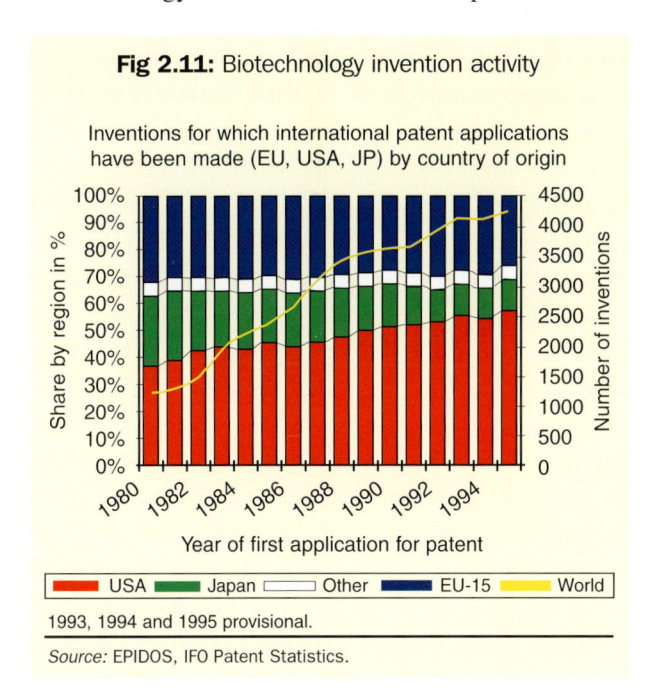

The results of the survey mentioned above indicate that the configuration of national innovation systems has a decisive influence on the generation of knowledge and the diffusion of technology. Different regulations within the innovation system favour some

---

[9] Benchmarking the Competitiveness of Biotechnology in Europe, June 1997

Chapter 3
Access to finance for European SMEs: a potential for growth and job creation

Small and Medium-sized Enterprises (SMEs) are extremely important for our economies, and not only because of their number. On the one hand, the intrinsic flexibility of most of them plays a major role in smoothing the ups and downs of the business cycle[1]. On the other hand, a very dynamic minority of SMEs represents a fundamental source of dynamism for the economy. These firms are widely considered as the driving force for high growth and stable job creation.

SMEs usually have much more restricted access to financial markets than Large Enterprises (LEs). This is particularly true in Europe because, although progress is being made towards having efficient risk-capital markets, the current situation represents a major shortcoming, especially for high-growth SMEs.

Shortage of finance for these SMEs often blocks their growth as well as their capacity to create jobs, which represents a major loss for the whole European economy. It is therefore crucial for Europe to unlock such an unexploited potential through an increased availability of appropriate finance and, in particular, of risk capital.

1. SMEs: a potential for job creation

In Europe, SMEs account for 99.8% of the total number of companies and for about 2/3 of total employment (see Table 3.1).

Table 3.1: Enterprises distributed by number of employees, EU, 1996

	SMEs very small (0-9)		SMEs Small (10-49)		SMEs Medium (50-249)		LEs (250+)	
Number (1000)	17285	93.0%	1105	5.9%	165	0.9%	35	0.2%
Employees (1000)	37000	33.2%	21110	18.9%	15070	13.5%	38220	34.3%

Source: ENSR (European Network for SME Research).

The population of SMEs lacks homogeneity in terms of technology orientation, prospects of growth, expected long-run returns and, last but not least, capacity to create jobs.

A small share of SMEs heavily contributes to job and wealth creation. These small (at least for a while after their creation), high-growth firms are usually technology-based (TBFs, for Technology-Based Firms, from now on). The big difference between young TBFs and other SMEs is, by definition, in *how much* they grow. Their difference with respect to LEs is in *how* they grow: LEs mainly grow by mergers and their contribution to net economic growth tends to be lower than for TBFs.

The impact of these high-growth TBFs on employment creation has been impressive in the USA. Between 1991 and 1995, 3% of firms (so-called 'gazelles' for their size and dynamism) accounted for 80% of job growth: 6 million new jobs out of the additional 7.7 million[2]. Further, the 5500 firms quoted in NASDAQ have created 16% of all new jobs in the USA in the first half of the nineties.

Actually, SMEs not only *create*, but also *destroy* jobs faster than larger firms do. They grow faster when they succeed but only about half of them survive their first five years. Nevertheless, the net flow of jobs created by SMEs remains positive.

This is especially true for TBFs which, according to several studies reported in an OECD survey[3], have higher than average survival rates. In addition, these high-tech, high-growth firms tend to create more stable (and highly qualified) jobs. They also generate positive technological spillovers and other positive externalities benefiting consumers as well as other producers.

---

[1] Dorothée Rivaud-Danset, *Comparisons between the financial structure of the SME versus large enterprises within the framework of the BACH database*, IDHE, June 1998.

[2] Cognetics, *Who's Creating Jobs*, 1995.
[3] OECD, *Technology, Productivity and Job Creation: Best Policy Practices*, 1998.

2. Access to finance for SMEs

Access to finance is a crucial issue for SMEs, even more than for LEs. This is mainly because SMEs are more subject than LEs to suffer some finance shortage: they have a narrower range of possibilities of external finance and in most cases they do not have enough own (or intra-group) funds to finance, for instance, innovative projects.

The necessity to finance the development of innovative, capital-intensive projects is exactly what makes external finance even more important for TBFs than for other SMEs, whose prime need may only be that for working capital (for instance, stocks).

Profitability

Profitability represents a broad indicator of a firm's self-financing capabilities[4].

Over the period 1986-1995[5], European SMEs recorded a systematically lower net profit ratio (i.e. the ratio of net profit on net turnover) than LEs (2.1% against 2.6%, see Fig. 3.1). This is however no surprise, since such a gap in performance traditionally increases during a period of expansion, as after 1993, and decreases during stagnation phases.

The performance of SMEs in the USA was better than that of European SMEs and, after a period of relative convergence during the late eighties, the gap in terms of net profitability has now become wider than ever.

Since 1993, economic expansion has helped firms to improve their profitability and, ceteris paribus, their self-financing capabilities. In addition, financial markets liberalisation has contributed to widen the range of external financial resources available to European firms.

This trend has been particularly true for LEs, which have displayed a significant trend towards debt reduction. On the contrary, European SMEs still show a persistent structural dependence on debt, especially on bank debt, considerably higher than for larger European firms.

Fig 3.1: Net profit ratio, EU-11, 1986–95, average

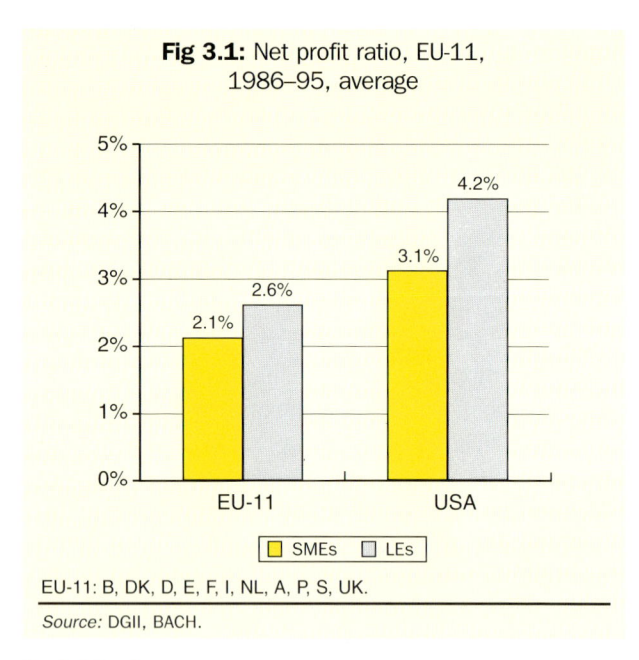

EU-11: SMEs 2.1%, LEs 2.6%
USA: SMEs 3.1%, LEs 4.2%

EU-11: B, DK, D, E, F, I, NL, A, P, S, UK.
Source: DGII, BACH.

Indebtedness

LEs have considerably reduced their indebtedness towards financial institutions, which dropped from 22.5% in 1986 to 10.8% in 1995 (see Fig. 3.2)[6].

Fig 3.2: Indebtness to financial institutions, EU-9, 1986-1995

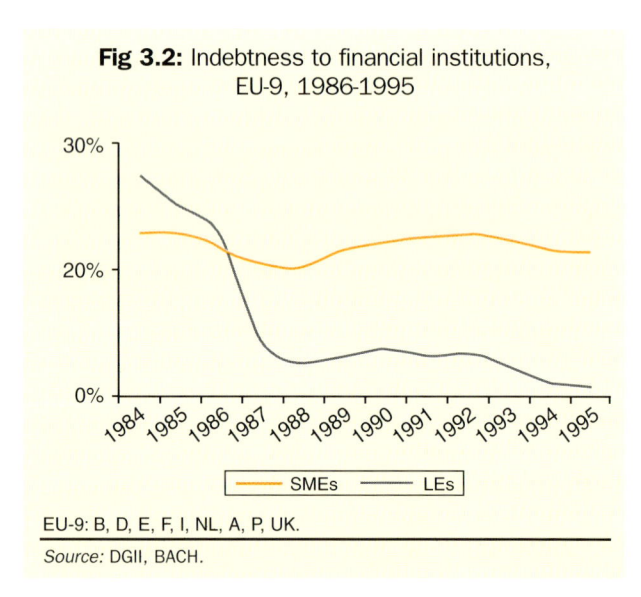

EU-9: B, D, E, F, I, NL, A, P, UK.
Source: DGII, BACH.

A better access of LEs to alternative sources of finance, such as capital markets (both national and international) has been the main driver of this trend. On the contrary, the stability of SMEs' financial indebtedness reflects the limited or even absence of access to most of the possibilities open to LEs.

Bank loans represent the major source of external finance for the vast majority of SMEs that have grown enough to satisfy traditional bank creditworthiness

---

[4] Internal finance available for investment also depends on firm's policy in the distribution of profits to stakeholders.
[5] *Financial situation of European enterprises,* European Economy, No. 7 (Supplement A), July 1997.
[6] Part of the drop observed in 1987 is due to the inclusion of German data.

criteria and to service the debt. These SMEs, as the traditional theory on small businesses suggests, consider alternative sources such as equity finance, only once internal sources and debt finance have been exhausted. Only 10% of European SMEs surveyed in 1996 were financed by external equity, while 49% had long-term loans, and 54% had overdrafts[7].

SMEs and banks

After the change in the bank-lending attitude of European LEs, SMEs have become the foundation of the customer base of European banks.

The relationship banks-SMEs is often very closely knitted, following the bank-centred tradition of most European financial systems. This type of relationship fits well for many established SMEs, which simply need a 'financial safety net' to face unexpected negative contingencies and seize sudden upturns in demand. High indebtedness, eventually with a predominant short-term maturity, and a low level of own resources may not be much of a problem for these SMEs. In fact, their focus is rather on the continuity of the flow of such (short-term) loans or, at least, on prompt availability.

However, there are several points that are sensitive in this relationship, especially as far as TBFs are involved. A recent round table of bankers and SMEs representatives[8] highlighted the different viewpoints.

The SME representatives believe that banks charge too much. This point is supported by a study of the Bank of England[9], which reports the existence in the UK of considerable differentials in loan rates by size classes of firms, with no evidence of any decreasing trend. Another study[10] of some European countries (Belgium, France, Germany, Italy and Spain) uses the apparent interest rate to estimate the risk premium supported by SMEs with respect to LEs. The study reports higher differentials (2-3%) for small firms than for medium-size firms (0-1%).

Another point raised by SMEs is that banks concentrate too much on risks and not enough on both the qualities of the entrepreneur and the future prospects for his business. This excessively risk-averse approach often drives banks to require unreasonably high collateral.

Banks feel that the main problem is how to conduct an effective and efficient relationship management policy. They argue that attention should be focused away from cost reduction towards client service with the ultimate goal of improving the quality of the relationship and the variety of services on offer.

This debate is far from coming to an end. It is nevertheless clear that banks can play a twofold role. They can keep on playing the usual role of financial safety net through a preferential, long-lasting relationship with established SMEs, which operate in mature sectors. But they have also the capability to play a new role, as far as they accept to adopt a more sophisticated approach to risk and secure a better provision of reasonably priced finance to promising TBFs.

3. High-growth SMEs: the role of risk-capital finance

Bank credit may be less important as a source of finance for TBFs, contrary to other SMEs.

For instance, apart from cost considerations, TBFs often find it difficult to provide the collateral that banks require for balancing TBFs' higher perceived risk. Since TBFs' assets are mainly intangible, access to bank lending in those cases relies exclusively on the owner's capacity to provide adequate collateral through his private wealth.

Risk capital (see Box 3.1) seems to be a more proper source of long-term funding for start-up and development of TBFs, whose internal resources are usually very limited with respect to planned investments. These firms are a minority of SMEs, as revealed by two UK surveys. A first survey reports that only 3% of external finance to small businesses in 1996 was in the form of equity[11], while a second survey reveals that only 1/3 of small businesses was prepared to take this form of financing into consideration[12]. Nonetheless, TBFs are a very important minority because of their dynamism and growth potential.

---

[7] *Grant Thornton Business Survey*, 1996.
[8] *The Second Round Table of Bankers and SMEs*, Final Report, DG XXIII of the EU Commission, February 1997.
[9] Bank of England, *Finance for Small Firms*, Fifth Report, Manor Park Press Ltd., Eastbourne, January 1998.
[10] Dorothée Rivaud-Danset, *Comparisons between the financial structure of the SME versus large enterprises within the framework of the BACH database*, IDHE, June 1998, p. 37.

[11] ESRC Cambridge Centre for business Research, *The changing state of British enterprise*, 1996.
[12] BCC (British Chambers of Commerce), *Small Firms Survey*, no. 24 (Finance), July 1997.

Box 3.1: Risk capital

'Risk capital' stands for equity financing to firms in the early growth stages of their lifecycle (namely, seed, start up and development). Buyout financing is often included, as far as Europe is concerned.

Risk capital encompasses both private equity investment and capital raised through secondary capital markets.

'Private equity' stands for investment in stakes of companies not listed on public stock markets. They can be separated in the following categories: '(formal) venture capital', i.e. stakes subscribed by either close-end funds ('venture capital funds') or other companies ('corporate venture capital'), and 'informal venture capital', i.e. stakes subscribed by individual investors (the so-called 'Business Angels').

'Second-tier stock exchanges' are mainly specialised in SMEs and high-growth companies. A non-previously listed company can start floating, eventually through an 'initial public offering' (IPO). In this way a company sells shares that are traded on the market for the first time and allows venture capitalists to dispose of the capital invested ('exit'). A listed company can raise additional equity capital by issuing shares to existing shareholders ('rights issue') or new investors ('cash offer').
The securities traded on public stock markets (either second-tier or primary) are 'public equities'.

A favourable context

European risk-capital markets are experiencing an upturn that, unlike previous boom-and-bust phases of the latest decade, looks more durable than ever.

From its creation until July 1998, EASDAQ (see Box 3.2) registered ECU 1.7 billion raised by firms through IPOs. Similarly, by November 1997, the Euro-NM network raised about ECU 880 million.

In addition, private equity markets have also shown an encouraging rise in activity, although with wide cross-country variance[13].

In 1996, the cumulated stock of funds raised by venture capital companies amounted to ECU 58.7 billion, more than double with respect to 1990 (see Fig. 3.3). The flow of new raised funds more than doubled in a decade: from ECU 2.8 billion in 1987 to ECU 6.7 billion in 1996.

The most developed venture capital market is in the UK. It accounts for more than 40% of European total, both in stock and flows. The Dutch market presented the most outstanding development between 1992 and 1996, reaching a level of new raised funds in 1996 (ECU 1.4 billion) second only to the UK. In 1997, that market did not maintain the same pace of development and Germany, with ECU 1.3 billion new funds (with an increase of 85% with respect to 1996), replaced the Netherlands at the second place. France is the second largest venture capital market in Europe for cumulated funds, dominated by closed-end funds (in 1996 there were 123 funds with total assets amounting to ECU 1.717 billion).

Fig 3.3: Venture capital – cumulative stock of funds raised, EU, 1990-1996

Year	ECU billion
1990	28.4
1991	33.0
1992	38.5
1993	40.5
1994	46.7
1995	49.7
1996	58.7

Source: EVCA.

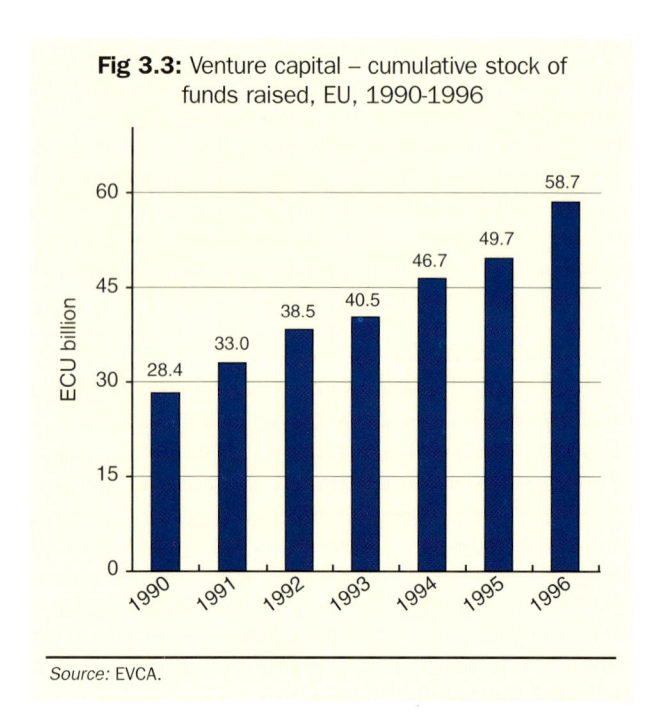

[13] Due to the weakness of available data on informal venture capital, most studies concentrate on formal venture capital. Some surveys broadly estimate that informal venture capital ranges between 4 and 8 times the amount of formal venture capital. Namely, 4 times for the UK, 4.15 times for the Netherlands, 7.44 times for Denmark and 7.73 times for the US (see *Innovation finance in Europe. A pilot project in benchmarking*, Bannock Consulting, 1998).

Box 3.2: Secondary stock exchanges

EASDAQ (European Association of Securities Dealers Automated Quotation System) is a pan-European quote-driven market modelled on NASDAQ (National Association of Securities Dealers Automated Quotation System). It started operations in September 1996 and targets medium-sized high-growth firms with an average market capitalisation of ECU 432 million.

Euro-NM, another pan-European market network of four national secondary markets (Paris, Brussels, Amsterdam and Frankfurt) targets European start-up TBFs. It was set up between February 1996 (Paris) and March 1997 (Frankfurt).

These two stock markets reflect two simultaneous trends that have been recently evident in Europe: the creation of a pan-European second-tier capital market (the EASDAQ) and a growing co-operation between some existing national stock markets (giving rise to the Euro-NM). They represent two facets of the same choice to operate on a Europe-wide basis. This is a reasonable answer to the necessity of achieving a higher level of activity in view of making Europe an attractive market for risk capital.

The UK AIM (Alternative Investment Market, London) differs from EASDAQ and Euro-NM under several aspects. This national (and not pan-European) stock market has a much more sizeable listing (but not a correspondingly higher capitalisation) and targets companies from a wider cross-section of businesses, ranging from TBFs to companies from more mature sectors. Nevertheless, TBFs account for more than 20% of the market.

These markets, with the exception of EASDAQ, are all complementary to primary markets. They are mainly intended to facilitate the transition of the most successful firms towards main capital market and, thus, will never experience a huge growth. The single authorities in charge of both markets have no interest in fostering competition. This is a major difference with respect to NASDAQ, which is an independent competitor to a main market. Many companies listed there are no longer SMEs, although they began that way, and are not willing to be listed on the main stock exchange. EASDAQ is also independently managed but 25 years younger than NASDAQ, which is certainly one reason for the much smaller listing.

Characteristics of European risk-capital market

Two major stylised facts characterise the European risk-capital market, as compared to the USA. First, different patterns of investment, less oriented towards the early stages of high-tech firms. Secondly, the relatively smaller level of activity (i.e. smaller listing and lower trade volumes) of secondary markets.

Data on the stage distribution of venture capital investment show that, as compared to the USA, European venture capitalists are more oriented towards investing in later stages of businesses, namely in the financing the expansion of an existing company. In 1997, venture capital channelled in the USA towards businesses in their early stages has been 4.3 times as much as in Europe, while for later stages it has been 'only' 1.9 times more (see Fig. 3.4).

This different investment pattern is even amplified when looking at the two phases of the early stage: 'seed' investment (i.e. financing the research to develop the initial idea) and the following 'start-up' investment (i.e. financing the product development and the initial marketing, before obtaining positive profits). In 1996, the USA provided 7.5 times more seed stage capital (see Table 3.2).

Fig 3.4: Venture capital – stage distribution of investment, Europe and USA, 1997

	EU	USA
Early stages	704	3030
Later stages	3912	7344

(ECU million)

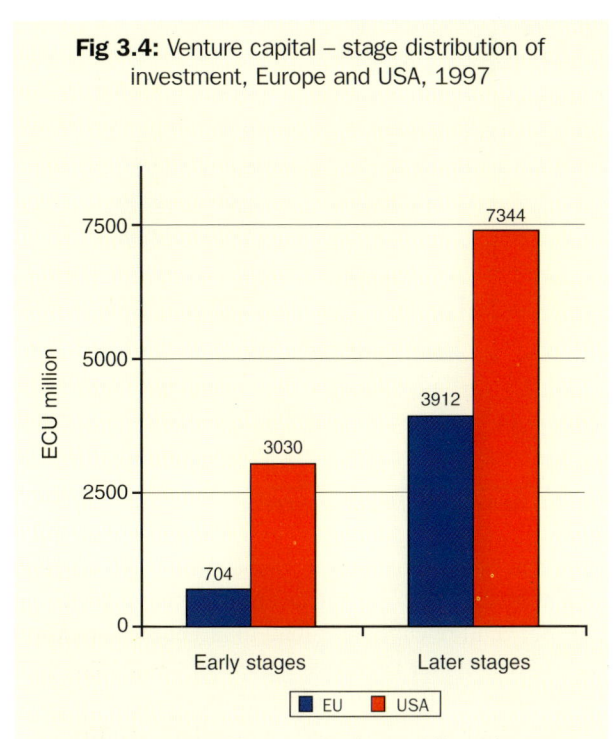

Later stages contain development and replacement. Buyout investments (about ECU 4.8 billion) are excluded for Europe to make data comparable with the USA.

Source: EVCA 1998 Yearbook and NVCA 1997 Annual Report; adjustments by Bannock Consulting.

CHAPTER 3

Table 3.2: Venture capital – investment distribution in early stage, Europe and USA, 1996

	EU-14 (ECU million)	USA (ECU million)	USA / EU-14
Seed	67	504	7.5
Start up and other early stage	751	2967	3.6
Total	818	3471	4.2

EU-14: EU except Luxembourg.

Source: EVCA, Venture Economics; adjustments by Bannock Consulting

A major reason for these different stage distributions probably lies in rates of return. In 1996, for instance, the internal rate of return of European venture capital funds focussed on early-stage investment was much lower (5.7%) than for other types of venture funds (see Fig. 3.5), as well as for early-stage investments in the USA (14.2%)[14]. This may derive from the lack of risk assessment skills and/or sophisticated financial intermediaries, from a higher rate of failure (eventually related to a lack of finance) and from a lack of information. All this might also depend on a general lack of networking among high-tech SMEs, research centres and financial circles.

Fig 3.5: Rates of return on investment by venture capital funds, EU, 1996

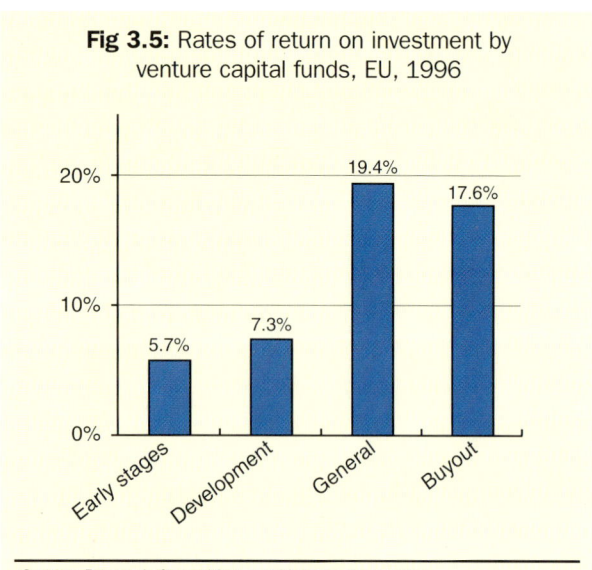

- Early stages: 5.7%
- Development: 7.3%
- General: 19.4%
- Buyout: 17.6%

Source: Bannock Consulting and Venture Economics.

Differences in the sector distribution of venture capital investments are consistent with that picture. In Europe, venture capitalists tend to target more mature sectors (consumer products, industrial equipment and machinery) while high-tech sectors (biotechnology, communications, computers and other electronics-related products) account for only 16% of total investments made in 1996 (see Fig. 3.6). In the same year in the USA, the computer software sector alone attracted 26.6% of the total.

These different patterns signal unfavourable conditions for early stage and technology-related investments in Europe, which definitely represent a key shortcoming for the promotion of rapid technological change, economic growth and job creation.

The second stylised fact is that the level of activity of European secondary stock markets (see Box 3.2) is still deemed insufficient, especially when compared to the USA (see Table 3.3).

Additional anecdotal evidence of an existing gap comes from the observation that European demand and supply of risk capital sometimes meet each other on NASDAQ. About hundred European SMEs are listed at NASDAQ and a number of major European institutional investors operating on NASDAQ tend to concentrate their investment on those European companies.

Fig 3.6: Venture capital – investment distribution by sector, EU and USA, 1996

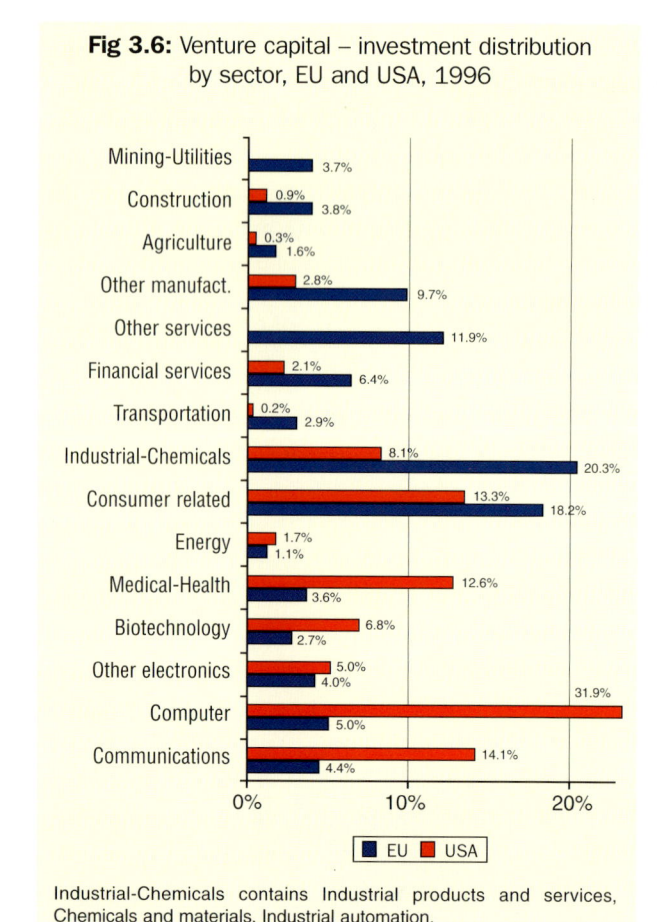

Sector	EU	USA
Mining-Utilities	—	3.7%
Construction	0.9%	3.8%
Agriculture	0.3%	1.6%
Other manufact.	2.8%	9.7%
Other services	—	11.9%
Financial services	2.1%	6.4%
Transportation	0.2%	2.9%
Industrial-Chemicals	8.1%	20.3%
Consumer related	13.3%	18.2%
Energy	1.7%	1.1%
Medical-Health	12.6%	3.6%
Biotechnology	6.8%	2.7%
Other electronics	5.0%	4.0%
Computer	31.9%	5.0%
Communications	14.1%	4.4%

Industrial-Chemicals contains Industrial products and services, Chemicals and materials, Industrial automation.

Source: EVCA, Venture Capital Journal.

---

[14] *International Investment Benchmark Report 1997*, Bannock Consulting, 1998.

Table 3.3: Secondary stock exchanges

	Date started	Listed	Market capitalisation (ECU billion)	Date of reference
EASDAQ	9/1996	38	16.37	7/1998
Euro-NM	2/96-3/97	57	5.34	11/1997
AIM	6/1995	308	8.51	12/1997
NASDAQ	1971	5393	1870.75	5/1998

Source: AIM, EASDAQ, Euro-NM, NASDAQ.

The relationship between the two aforementioned stylised facts goes through the strict interconnection between the two parts of the risk-capital market: private equities and secondary stock markets (see Box 3.1).

Private equities require an effective exit route, which is usually provided by the secondary stock market. A thin stock market (i.e. with insufficient listings and traded volumes) tends to deter venture capitalists, at least because they might have difficulties in disposing of their investment in a reasonable delay. Without an effective exit route, even when they invest, they are not ready to support the high risk implicit in early-stage investment for high-tech projects. This is an explanation for the difference in investment patterns between Europe and USA, in addition to differentials in rates of return.

This is one facet of the relationship between the two stylised facts. The other one is that a stock market requires a 'supply of firms' suitable and willing to be listed. But the lack of venture capital (or even the low risk propensity of investors) is likely to limit the emergence of new candidates for listing and, in the end, the development of the stock market.

Taken together, the two stylised facts reflect the reason why the development of risk-capital markets in Europe is still not satisfactory: there is not enough risk capital and, even that smaller amount, is not channelled towards high-growth projects to which it should naturally be devoted.

On the other hand, the circularity of the relationship reveals that building an efficient risk-capital market is a matter of simultaneously developing (or even creating) a set of mutually dependent entities as well as the reciprocal trust that each one will fulfil its task whenever called upon. This process takes time, for instance to achieve sufficiently high standards of disclosure and transparency, and it will last longer the more (institutional, regulatory, etc.) barriers there are and the less (public and private) effort is devoted in removing them.

In addition, developing an efficient risk-capital market is a matter of supply of risk capital as well as of demand. Demand for risk capital comes from firms with specific financial needs, mainly due to their orientation towards growth and innovation. Supply of risk capital comes from individuals, institutional investors (e.g. pension funds) as well as other firms.

4. Remaining barriers

A number of remaining obstacles slows down the transition towards an appropriate provision (supply) and use (demand) of risk capital. A European benchmarking study on the financing of innovation[15] and a report by the EU Commission[16] provide some guidance in the identification of these remaining barriers.

On the demand side, the legal and regulatory environment represents a first obstacle[17]. In many European countries, the administrative procedures for setting up and registering a new company are burdensome and expensive.

A second barrier comes from the fragmentation of European financial markets. On the most restrictive definition, the EU still counts 33 stock exchanges and 18 controlling organisms. From listed firms' viewpoint, this brings about different accounting standards, disclosure requirements, as well as company law and tax regimes. This often makes cross-border capital raising initiatives more difficult than they already are, especially for SMEs, and in the end negatively affect risk-capital demand.

Finally, many European tax systems have been deemed not to be conducive to company creation. For instance, a more favourable tax treatment of R&D expenditure is likely to favour high-tech start-ups and, thus, demand of risk capital.

On the supply side, a major obstacle is the persistent shortage of risk-assessment skills (see Box 3.3). The presence of sophisticated investors, capable to evaluate high-risk (and high-tech) projects, depends on the attractiveness of the market. The level of activity of European markets just starts justifying such an interest.

---

[15] *Innovation finance in Europe. A pilot project in benchmarking*, Bannock Consulting, 1998.
[16] *Risk Capital: A Key to Job Creation in the European Union*, Communication of the EU Commission, April 1998.
[17] The elimination of unnecessary administrative burden is one *major objective of the Report of the Business Environment Simplification Task force*, BEST, 1998.

Banks would have the potential to provide such skills, but the European bank-centred financial tradition justified banks' inertia. Only recently, under growing competitive pressure, have banks started to move in this direction. Creating these skills requires time for both sophisticated investors and banks. The late start of Europe is one major reason for the present shortage.

The regulatory framework represents an obstacle also on the supply side. In particular, the constraints to investment in risk capital by pension funds are much tighter in Europe than in the USA. In Europe (with the notable exception of UK and Netherlands) 'asset restriction' (i.e. restriction to the extent of investment in non-quoted companies) is generally imposed.

Box 3.3: Limiting the risk of high-risk projects

A new project contains an element of intrinsic risk because expected results of research may not be attained and marketing of products may come out to be unsuccessful.

From investor's viewpoint, this technological and commercial risk becomes less relevant, the lower the share of each project in the whole investment portfolio. In fact, as traditional risk-diversification arguments suggest, investing in high-risk projects may become a safe activity as far as the overall investment is spread over a sufficiently wide range of investment opportunities with independent risks.

This is why it is important that investors have the choice among a wide range of (uncorrelated) deals available.

In addition, trade volumes are also relevant. Higher market liquidity tends to drive down the volatility of share prices as well as to prevent investors' fear of being unable to sell their shares because of low demand.

Risk capital would therefore benefit from a high degree of skill available in the market (i.e. sophistication in the assessment, management and monitoring of risk), high standards of information disclosure by firms, high levels of activity and transparency of markets.

In the USA, on the contrary, no explicit constraint is imposed other than a generic 'prudent man rule' (i.e. the legitimate expectation that fund managers will behave as careful professionals). Lifting the constraints on European pension funds would be a sensible choice, on grounds of traditional portfolio differentiation arguments (see Box 3.3), and it is likely to considerably increase the provision of risk capital.

Finally, tax treatment in Europe, as compared to the USA, is less conducive to risk-capital supply. Some of the major items concerned are preferential tax treatment of capital gains and tax incentives to promote schemes of equity pay (and/or of employee ownership).

Part Two

The European manufacturing industry

Chapter 4
Competitiveness and sectoral development: building the links

The purpose of the second part of the report is to identify strengths and weaknesses in competitive performance by looking at the current patterns and changes in the structure of European manufacturing. The analysis is based upon the assumption that competitiveness, structural development and standard of living are strongly interlinked phenomena. Within this context, the term 'structural' refers exclusively to the distribution of production across sectors and industries.[1]

After presenting evidence of the differences in the specialisation patterns within the EU, the subsequent chapters (a) investigate the impact of structural development on growth and employment potentials; (b) provide basic referential data on European competitive performance relative to Japan and the USA; and (c) try to identify underlying forces and broad patterns in the strategic behaviour of firms by applying a new industry typology. The results will be interpreted in the context of economic predictions on structure and specialisation in a high wage economy.

1. Outline of the analysis

The second part of the report is organised as follows:
1. *Competitiveness and sectoral development - building the links:* The introductory chapter describes international specialisation patterns in industrial production. Theories on growth, international trade and investment as well as industrial organisation are screened for relevant hypotheses. In this way, a broad analytical framework for structural analysis can be developed.

2. *Sectoral growth, employment and productivity:* The focus of Chapter 5 is on *internal performance* - i.e. the sectoral contributions to growth in income, employment and consumption. After summarising the major trends and growth patterns at the sectoral level, the relationship between economic growth and employment at the industry level is tested. This reveals significant differences between the EU, Japan and the USA. These differences extend to the sources of growth in labour productivity: shifts in the sectoral composition of output appear to have a substantial impact in Europe and Japan, but not in the USA.

3. *European industries in world markets:* Chapter 6 examines the EU's position in the global marketplace, with particular emphasis on international market shares and trade balances. Comparisons with Japan and the USA provide benchmarks for evaluating relative strengths and weaknesses. The specific nature of trade data allows a distinction to be made between competition based purely on prices and competition based primarily on quality and product differentiation. For example, the data reveal that the EU enjoys a considerable quality premium in its trade relationship.

4. *Industrial specialisation and performance:* To improve the economic relevance of sectoral analysis, a new typology of industries is created, based on typical factor input combinations and using statistical cluster techniques. The analysis illustrates that the EU is locked into rather traditional industries, characterised by high levels of labour input and physical capital. The EU is lagging behind the USA in the fastest moving markets, in which competition is characterised by investment in intangible assets, such as marketing and innovation.

5. *Global investment and multinational firms:* In addition to growing trade, foreign direct investment and multinational activity are the primary driving forces of global economic integration. At the same time, casual evidence based on observations in large multinational firms suggests a tendency towards reducing diversification and a return to core businesses. Drawing on a unique data set, Chapter 8 examines these trends in more detail. A pronounced increase in intra-EU multinational activity is identified but

---
[1] Throughout the analysis higher aggregated levels corresponding to NACE 2-digits will be referred to as 'sectors', while the term 'industry' will be used for lower aggregations corresponding to NACE 3-digits.

the tendency to revert to the core business turns out to be weaker than expected. Furthermore, foreign direct investments are found to be driven mainly by the objectives of market access and exploitation of knowledge-based assets.

6. *Competitive strengths and weaknesses of European manufacturing - Summary and conclusions:* The second part of the report presents a range of perspectives on and approaches to the analysis of structural development and competitive performance. The final summary attempts to draw a number of distinct lines of argument together and to give a short and concise assessment of the major strengths and weaknesses of European industry. The general policy implications are sketched and support an overall emphasis on horizontal measures fostering productivity and growth, rather than on sectoral targeting.

Table 4.1: Sectoral shares in manufacturing value added 1995 in %

	EU	Japan	USA	Total
Food, Beverages & Tobacco	11.60	9.83	11.90	11.23
Textiles, Clothing & Leather	5.38	4.12	4.38	4.63
Wood, Pulp & Paper	5.10	4.54	6.26	5.40
Publishing & Printing	5.00	6.18	7.33	6.25
Refined Petroleum	3.11	1.49	1.55	2.04
Chemicals	11.45	10.94	12.70	11.80
Rubber, Plastic Products	4.59	5.07	4.39	4.65
Non-metalic Mineral Products	4.57	4.50	2.62	3.78
Basic Metals	4.74	5.08	3.85	4.48
Fabricated Metal	6.97	6.69	5.50	6.31
Machinery, Other Fab. Metal	10.92	11.71	9.04	10.40
Office Machinery	1.53	2.66	2.55	2.25
Electrical Machinery	5.47	5.13	3.15	4.46
Radio, TV & Communication	3.09	7.78	6.09	5.59
Precision Instruments	2.51	1.91	4.84	3.26
Motor Vehicles	8.57	8.16	7.07	7.86
Other Transport	2.50	1.93	3.79	2.85
Other Manufacturing	2.90	2.26	2.96	2.75

Source: DEBA; WIFO calculations.

2. The international division of labour

Reflecting the Ricardian notion of *comparative* advantage, *absolute* advantages across all industries are neither achievable nor desirable for an economy. In each location, certain industries must be more efficient than others in the use of productive resources. The international division of labour and foreign trade then creates mutual benefits from the distinct patterns of industrial specialisation. On this basis, a broad description of the international division of labour is provided as a general background.

The global division of labour: EU, Japan and USA

The specialisation patterns of the EU, Japan and the USA exhibit a high degree of similarity at the more aggregate sectoral levels but reveal considerable differences when further disaggregated into individual industries. This is in line with trade theory, which predicts that developed nations will eventually switch from specialisation governed by exogenous endowments to specialisation governed by differentiated firm strategies, enabling first mover advantages and the formation of industrial clusters.

With the notable exception of radio, TV and communication equipment, where in 1995 shares in the EU (3%) lagged considerably behind those in the USA (6%) and in Japan (8%), the distribution of shares in total value added measured at the sectoral level is relatively even (see Table 4.1).

However, a higher degree of differentiation in the composition of output emerges when individual industries are examined. Relative specialisation in production is measured by the ratio of a specific industry's value added in the share of a particular country's total manufacturing relative to the same ratio which the EU, Japan and the USA are taken together (see Fig. 4.1). The following examples demonstrate the diversity that typically emerges within sectors:

- In the electronics sector, the EU has the greatest degree of specialisation relative to Japan and the USA, in the production of wire and cable and electrical apparatus. Japan shows a clear profile of specialisation in electronic consumer goods, for example audio-visual apparatus, watches and clocks, as well as electronic components. The USA has its greatest strength in advanced applications of information and communication technologies (ICTs) such as medical equipment, precision instruments and optical instruments.

- With regard to transportation vehicles, the EU is most specialised in the manufacture of railway and motor vehicles. Compared to the total of the three economic areas, Japan has its highest shares of value added in motorcycles and bicycles, as well as in motor vehicle parts. The USA is most specialised in aircraft and spacecraft.

- Within textiles and clothing, the EU is most specialised in textile fibres and the processing of leather and fur, while Japan specialises in the finishing of textiles and in knitted and crocheted fabrics. The USA appears to be markedly specialised only in textile articles.

Fig. 4.1: Industries with top shares in value added relative to the total of EU-Japan-USA 1995

EU
Ceramic tiles & flags
Construction materials
Leather clothes
Recorded media
Steam generators
Footwear
Dressing of leather
Textile fibres
Railway vehicles
Knitted & crocheted articles
Isolated wire & cable
Articles of fur
Cement, lime & plaster
Luggage, handbags, etc.
Motor vehicles

USA
Aircraft & spacecraft
Grain mill products
Medical equipment
Sports goods
Electronic components
Precisions instruments
Agro-chemical products
Tobacco products
Optical instruments
Bodies for motor vehicles
Weapons & ammunition
Made-up textile articles
Other mineral products
Pulp, paper & paperboard
Cutlery, tools & hardware

JAPAN
Motorcycles & bicycles
Fish & fish products
Processing of stone
Musical instruments
Knitted fabrics
Audio-visual apparatus
Watches & clocks
Other wood & cork products
Domestic appliances
Parts for motor vehicles
Electrical equipment
Structural metal products
Electronic components
Accumulators & batteries
Finishing of textiles

Source: DEBA; WIFO calculations.

Specialisation within the EU

Most of the following analysis will treat Europe as one single economic area. It is, nevertheless, worthwhile considering the broad patterns of specialisation across the Member States as these show some interesting features. Listing the top 5 industries with the highest shares in value added relative to the EU total reveals some pronounced country specific advantages and particular success stories of industrial locations within the EU (see Fig. 4.2). For example, in interpreting the patterns, different endowments of natural resources can easily be recognised as the underlying causes of the high share of saw milling, planing and impregnation of wood, pulp and paper in Sweden and Finland, articles of wood and cork in Portugal, and fish products in Denmark. In addition, the high relative shares of apparel, luggage, handbags and footwear, tanning and articles of fur, and similar products in Portugal, Spain, Italy and Greece indicate comparative advantages with regard to labour costs. On the other hand, specific demand conditions can e.g. account for

the specialisation in the manufacture of ships and boats in Denmark and the UK.

Besides these examples, the specialisation patterns observed strongly indicate the existence of location-specific pools of technological knowledge and marketing skills, and, accordingly, of cluster dynamics, generated and magnified by the interplay of historical circumstances, entrepreneurial achievements and locational advantages[2]. Particular examples may be the high share of food processing and games and toys in Denmark; agro-chemical products, food processing, and aircraft and spacecraft in the UK; power generation or typical marketing industries, such as sports goods, detergents, cleaning agents and perfumes in France; communication technologies in both Sweden and Finland; consumer electronics in the Netherlands; and various types of electrical and mechanical machinery in Germany. Finally, Ireland is a special case, since its top 5 industries (with the highest relative shares in value added) strongly reflect the 'youth' of such products as office machinery and recorded media, the production of which was recently located there through an inflow of foreign direct investment.

3. Competitive performance and industrial structure

Specialisation and differentiated patterns of industrial production reflect what economic theory suggests will appear, given open markets and free trade on the one hand, and an uneven distribution of comparative advantage or economies of scale on the other.

Beyond these descriptive observations, two key questions lie at the heart of the analysis. Firstly, do the observable specialisation patterns provide clues as to the underlying strengths and weaknesses of economic performance, such as the ability to innovate and adapt to fast changing environments? Secondly, do they make a difference in terms of long term prospects for growth, employment and general welfare in an economy? In other words, does it matter that the EU is particularly specialised in industries such as mineral products or textiles and clothing whereas the USA is specialised in air- and spacecraft or medical equipment, and Japan in a number of electronic industries?

---

[2] Peneder, M., *Creating a Coherent Design for Cluster Analysis and Related Policies,* WIFO, 1997 (forthcoming in OECD proceedings).

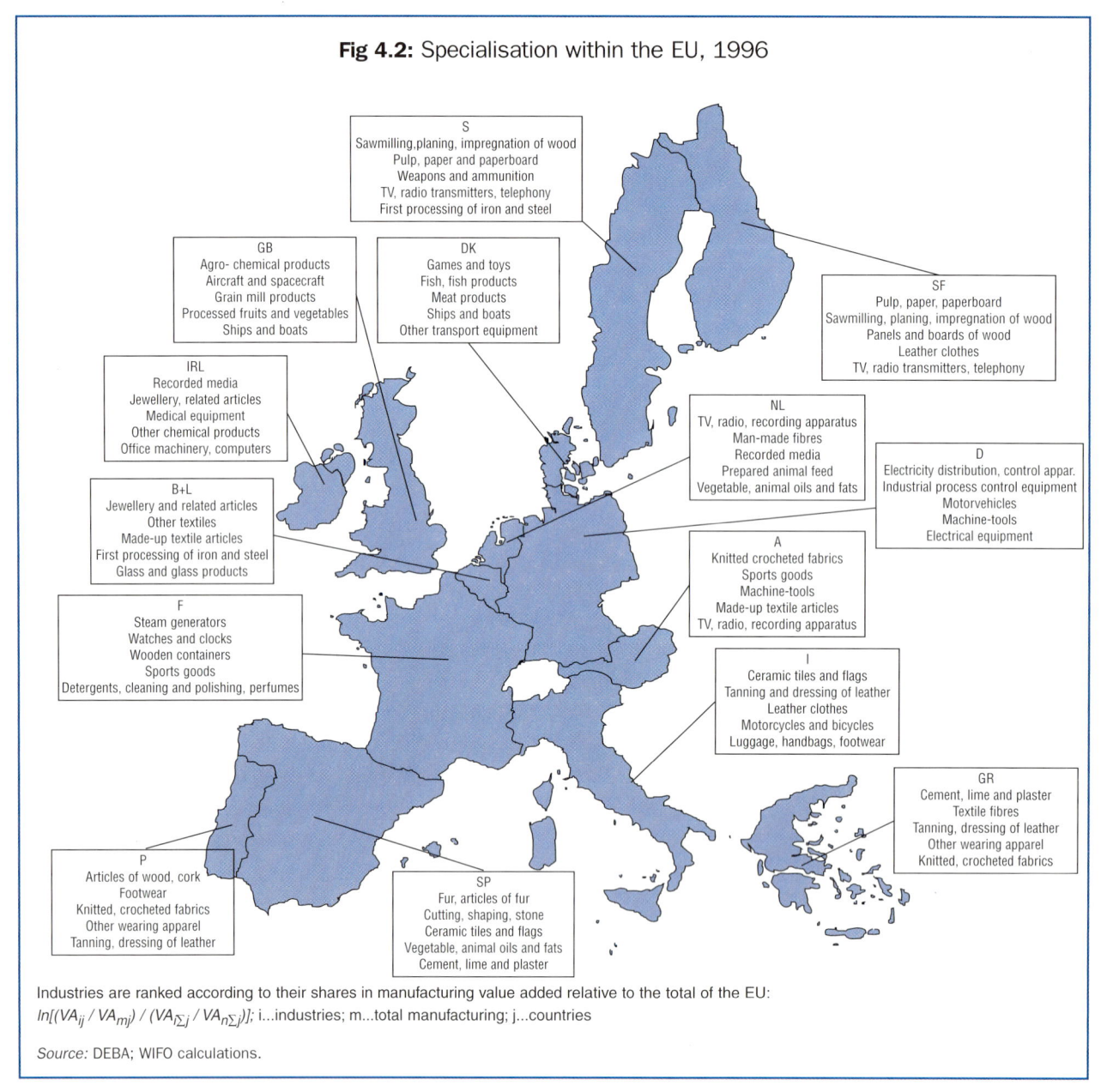

Fig 4.2: Specialisation within the EU, 1996

S
Sawmilling, planing, impregnation of wood
Pulp, paper and paperboard
Weapons and ammunition
TV, radio transmitters, telephony
First processing of iron and steel

GB
Agro- chemical products
Aircraft and spacecraft
Grain mill products
Processed fruits and vegetables
Ships and boats

DK
Games and toys
Fish, fish products
Meat products
Ships and boats
Other transport equipment

SF
Pulp, paper, paperboard
Sawmilling, planing, impregnation of wood
Panels and boards of wood
Leather clothes
TV, radio transmitters, telephony

IRL
Recorded media
Jewellery, related articles
Medical equipment
Other chemical products
Office machinery, computers

NL
TV, radio, recording apparatus
Man-made fibres
Recorded media
Prepared animal feed
Vegetable, animal oils and fats

D
Electricity distribution, control appar.
Industrial process control equipment
Motorvehicles
Machine-tools
Electrical equipment

B+L
Jewellery and related articles
Other textiles
Made-up textile articles
First processing of iron and steel
Glass and glass products

A
Knitted crocheted fabrics
Sports goods
Machine-tools
Made-up textile articles
TV, radio, recording apparatus

F
Steam generators
Watches and clocks
Wooden containers
Sports goods
Detergents, cleaning and polishing, perfumes

I
Ceramic tiles and flags
Tanning and dressing of leather
Leather clothes
Motorcycles and bicycles
Luggage, handbags, footwear

GR
Cement, lime and plaster
Textile fibres
Tanning, dressing of leather
Other wearing apparel
Knitted, crocheted fabrics

P
Articles of wood, cork
Footwear
Knitted, crocheted fabrics
Other wearing apparel
Tanning, dressing of leather

SP
Fur, articles of fur
Cutting, shaping, stone
Ceramic tiles and flags
Vegetable, animal oils and fats
Cement, lime and plaster

Industries are ranked according to their shares in manufacturing value added relative to the total of the EU:
$ln[(VA_{ij} / VA_{mj}) / (VA_{i\Sigma j} / VA_{n\Sigma j})]$; i...industries; m...total manufacturing; j...countries

Source: DEBA; WIFO calculations.

These questions are inherently related to the notion of competitiveness. The term competitiveness essentially deals with the performance of individual firms, while at the level of aggregate economies, the broader concept of competitive performance is more appropriate.

The first part of the report has singled out growth, job creation and rising productivity as the three core elements that influence an economy's prospects of increasing its standard of living.

The clear target is to optimise the overall standard of living, consistent with sustainable development. This is what is meant by an economy's *"ability to produce goods and services that meet the test of international markets while our citizens enjoy a standard of living that is both rising and sustainable"*[3].

As the preceding figures illustrate, distinct economic areas differ with regard to the sectoral distribution of production. Moreover, industries themselves may also differ with regard to their potential contributions to the achievement of a society's desired macroeconomic goals. Industries may exhibit different prospects for overall growth in demand, income, employment and productivity, for example. They may also differ with regard to their ability to generate positive externalities

---

[3] Tyson, L., *Who's bashing whom? Trade conflict in high-technology industries*, Institute for International Economics, Washington D.C., 1993. A similar definition is provided in Aiginger, K., 'A framework for evaluating the dynamic competitiveness of countries', *Structural Change and Economic Dynamics*, No 9, 1998, pp. 159-188.

to other industries via flows of tacit knowledge, common pools of specific labour and vertical supply relationships. Finally, their exposure to pure price competition and the global pressure on factor incomes and wage levels in particular may differ according to distinct degrees of homogeneity in product markets.

The combination of (i) differences in the sectoral composition of output, and (ii) differences across industries in their potential contribution to economic welfare builds the link between sectoral analysis on the one hand and competitive performance on the other. It is also the motivation for the kind of structural analysis carried out here. Empirical observations across industries help to map the major sources of strength and weakness across European manufacturing industries. They also help to demonstrate that the economy is an interlocking system in which policy must be customised according to specific needs, reflecting current structures as well as desired directions of future development.

4. Factors determining industrial structure

Economic theory currently does not provide a uniform framework for assessing which kind of industrial structure is most suitable for generating sustainable high incomes and employment. However, for the purpose of the analysis, three broad analytical criteria are identified. In short, industrial structures are presumed to be beneficial to overall economic performance the more they

- support the accumulation of knowledge and create positive externalities,

- correspond to the distribution of comparative advantage and dynamic economies of scale, and

- allow for product differentiation and investment in firm specific assets like innovation and marketing.

Spillovers and the accumulation of knowledge

Growth theory investigates which factors determine the growth path of nations and why growth rates differ. Although aggregate models are by definition not designed to provide predictions for structural developments, many underlying assumptions have found their way into sectoral analysis and shaped the way of thinking about factors of growth and structural change.

A particularly important aspect in the context of this report concerns the accumulation of knowledge and the extent of positive externalities[4]: In the absence of continuous technological progress, the mere accumulation of physical capital is assumed to exhibit diminishing returns. This generates the pessimistic prediction that the mere investment of physical capital in mature economies eventually causes per capita growth to cease. However, this is not the case when inputs are invested in knowledge, since no general assumption of diminishing returns applies to knowledge creation. On the contrary, the specific characteristics of knowledge accumulation and accordingly of moves upward on the learning curve even suggest increasing returns, allowing endogenous, sustainable growth in per capita income. In addition, knowledge usually is not perfectly appropriable and non-rival in its use. Thus, being close to public goods, knowledge spillovers to other producers work against the general tendency of diminishing returns in physical capital as well.

The main implication for structural analysis is that industries investing more in knowledge creation can also be expected to contribute more than others to the overall prospects for sustainable growth in the economy. From this perspective, the share of technically sophisticated industries can be monitored as an important indicator of economic growth potential. However, no clear prediction on the growth enhancing effects of the creation of knowledge spillovers emerges, since the acceleration of knowledge diffusion also reduces the to invest in R&D.

Comparative advantages and dynamic economies of scale

Trade theory explains the causes and the direction of trade, forecasting how countries specialise under equilibrium conditions. Equilibrium implies that all factors are fully utilised, trade balances are zero and product prices are equalised. The most fundamental prediction for the analysis of structural development is that the specialisation pattern in trade follows the distribution of comparative cost advantages. This is determined by differences in available technologies (*Ricardo*) or by the endowment with general (*Heckscher-Ohlin*) and sector specific (*Ricardo-Viner*) production factors.

However, traditional trade theory can only explain *inter-industry* trade between differently endowed or productive economic areas. A large proportion of international trade flows originates from sources other

---

[4] Aghion, P., Howitt, P., *Endogenous Growth Theory*, MIT Press, Cambridge, MA, 1998.

than comparative advantage, especially those between similar trading partners. This intra-industry trade also shapes industrial structures.

In markets characterised by product differentiation, each country limits itself to the production and export of a limited number of varieties or certain quality segments. Within these segments, firms are able to produce at sufficiently high volumes and exploit internal and external economies of scale. In a dynamic perspective, economies of scale additionally generate self-reinforcing feedback mechanisms, path dependency and - like a "*river that digs its own bed deeper*"[5] - first mover advantages come into existence. Lead-time then enables fast moving firms to top the learning curve and reinforce the productivity advantage. Cluster effects based on external economies of scale within a certain location then broaden and foster such specialisation.

The most direct implication for structural analysis would be the ineffectiveness of policy interventions, designed in negligence of the actual distribution of comparative advantages and inherited specialisation based on dynamic economies of scale.

Product differentiation

Industrial organisation describes the optimising behaviour of firms, taking into account strategic interactions within specific markets. Equilibrium is assumed insofar as demand equals supply, and a firm's decision proves optimal given the available information about the actions of other firms. Research in this area focuses mainly on the performance of firms and of markets (prices are related to marginal costs). Many factors are important: the variables to be set (available strategies), the mode of conduct, the time horizon of strategic interaction, the information structure and specific institutional settings like the severity of antitrust legislation.

Perhaps the most fundamental distinction in models of industrial organisation concerns the degree of product differentiation: in homogenous markets, competition drives down profits and prices to a uniform level, and production shifts to the competitor with the lowest unit costs. In contrast, heterogeneous markets allow firms to create the surplus necessary for covering the fixed costs of investments in e.g. innovation, vertical product differentiation, marketing and design. Firms in high wage countries can continue to survive by upgrading quality and introducing new process and product innovations. In such an environment, firms are able to supply products, which are less sensitive to prices, and thereby create a basis for maintaining high factor incomes.

The degree of product differentiation in a market does not necessarily arise from a 'natural' exogenously predetermined magnitude. In the first place, profit maximising firms locate themselves in the most profitable market niches and try to differentiate their products as much as possible from their competitors. Secondly, as Sutton (1991)[6] has pointed out, in advertising- and research-intensive industries, such investments are best interpreted as an endogenous variable within the strategic interaction of firms. In these industries, investment in response to newly entering firms shapes the structure of markets. In a particular market, endogenous sunk costs determine the amount of fixed capital expenditures spent on research and advertising and thus define the height of the entry barriers in a particular market.

Beyond the strict model focusing on the explanation of market structure, the inherent dynamic economies of scale in these industries suggest that the firm specific advantages thus created can foster and deepen industrial specialisation patterns over time.

Firm specific assets and multinational enterprises

Multinational investment is a key driving force in the international relocation of production and thus an important determinant of European industrial structure. In addition to location specific comparative advantages, multinational investment is motivated by the exploitation of firm specific assets. Individual enterprises develop their competitive strengths by accumulating technological and organisational knowledge, or by brand creation and reputation. Often, they are able to exploit these assets more efficiently within their organisation, rather than through arms length trade, such as selling licences or franchise agreements. For successful firms, constraints on growth in the home market additionally create important push factors for the expansion of activities into foreign markets.

---

[5] Krugman, P., *Rethinking International Trade*, MIT Press, Cambridge, MA, 1991.

[6] Sutton, J., *Sunk Costs and Market Structure*, MIT Press, Cambridge, MA, 1991. Sutton shows that in markets with *exogenous sunk costs* (entry costs or costs defined by minimum efficient scale) increasing the market size leads to fragmentation, in markets in which goodwill, advertising or research and development are important, the number of firms will not increase with market size.

Firm specific assets generate multi-plant economies of scale, which tend to make suchinvestments more profitable than in single plant firms.
It can therefore be expected that MNEs not only shape industrial structure by relocating production, but also generate additional productivity advantages as firms grow and endogenously invest in these firm specific assets.

The relationship between exports and FDI is a significant determinant of the contribution of foreign direct investment to employment, structural development and growth. Based on the proximity/plant size trade-off, a substitution-type relationship implies the delocation of production. A complementary relationship on the other hand strengthens the performance of industries and may even create new jobs in both the home and the host countries. The general pattern is expected to differ according to industry characteristics, form (vertical vs. horizontal FDI) and motives (cost efficiency, market access, strategy) for FDI. Firms also invest abroad for strategic reasons and engage in merger and acquisition activities. Although no additional production capacity is created, the impact on market structure and intensity of competition may be significant.

Finally, multinational activity is also motivated by specialisation within the organisation of firms. Within their own organisations, multinationals increasingly spread production stages across countries, according to the comparative advantages of the host countries. This new division of labour within multinational firms intensifies the competition among locations for the most attractive parts in the value-added chain.

The common theme

The overall focus of the analysis is on structural development and competitive performance, i.e. the relative strengths and weaknesses of European manufacturing across industries. Obviously, the selected economic theories mentioned above are not intended to form the basis for strict econometric testing of particular hypotheses. Instead, they provide the broad analytical framework, which shapes the different perspectives, angles of perception and deliberate choices in the analysis that follows.

Drawing together some major threads of and insights from economic theory on growth, trade, international investment and industrial organisations, an important distinction between the different sources of competitive advantage and structural development emerges. On the one hand, the sectoral distribution of industrial production is shaped by current or historic differences in 'natural' advantages, in the sense of exogenously given factors. On the other hand, advantages may be 'strategic' in the sense of being endogenously raised by targeted investment.

'Strategic' advantages deserve special attention, since such forms of purposeful investment are sensitive to public policy. In the subsequent chapters, therefore, the structural analysis is intended to raise awareness of two different poles in the spectrum of policy instruments. Policy can either emphasise low costs and low factor prices or concentrate on the capability to produce at the higher ends of a differentiated bandwidth of perceived quality. While both aspects must be pursued simultaneously, the option that ultimately receives greatest emphasis can be decisive in determining the dynamic prospects of an economy.

Chapter 5
Sectoral growth, employment and productivity

The empirical assessment of structural development has been split into the two dimensions of internal and external performance. While the latter deals directly with external exchange relationships via trade or foreign direct investment (both are investigated in subsequent chapters), internal performance is understood as the ability of an economic area to achieve the macroeconomic goals of growth in income, employment and consumption. Certainly, both dimensions are interlinked, since external relationships also contribute to income and employment.

This chapter is organised as follows: First of all, the size of manufacturing and the major trends in demand, industrial production and employment are investigated at the sectoral level. Secondly, panel regression tests the relationship between economic growth and employment at the industry level, with respect to significant differences between the EU, Japan and the USA. Finally, decomposition techniques are used to investigate the impact of structural change on labour productivity.

1. Overall trends

In general, the analysis focuses on differences in size and dynamics across industries within manufacturing. However, a few remarks on the development of total manufacturing are provided in order to put the results into a broader perspective.

Manufacturing produces about one fifth of the European gross domestic product. Over time, the share decreases slightly, mainly as a result of two occurrences: First of all, higher productivity leads to lower prices, notably in high tech areas such as new information and communication technologies. Secondly, as the degree of outsourcing increases, manufacturing becomes the source of booming industry-related services. Business services are among the few areas in which employment is increasing over time. Many of these jobs are inherently related to innovation, marketing, product differentiation and restructuring in manufacturing.

The share of manufacturing value added in GDP is larger in Europe (20.6%) than in the USA (18.0%), but lower than in Japan (24.7%)[1]. Comparing absolute size, the USA has the largest industrial sector, producing 41.5% of the common manufacturing value added, while the EU follows in second place with 32.8%, and Japan supplies slightly more than one quarter.

Taking the EU, Japan and the USA together, demand[2] for manufacturing grew by an average of 2.5% p.a. between 1989 and 1996 (see Table 5.1). The two most rapidly growing sectors are both related to information and communication technologies, namely radio, TV and communication equipment and office machinery. Demand has also grown rapidly in rubber and plastic products, motor vehicles, and publishing and printing. Food and beverages and chemicals contributed substantially to overall demand growth in absolute terms. Low growth rates or almost stagnant demand have been experienced in clothing, leather products, and precision instruments. The demand for products from the textile, other transport and basic metals sectors has been in absolute decline.

Comparing the dynamics of apparent consumption, the most significant differences are in office machinery, where the USA (7.7%) exhibits particularly strong and rising demand for information technology, outperforming Japan (6.6%) and far ahead of the EU (2.3%). At the same time, the US market shows a decline in the apparent consumption of other transport (-3.8%), as well as refined petroleum (-3.0%). With regard to the basic metals industry, the fastest decline in demand was in the EU (-1.7%).

---

[1] The numbers are from OECD (*National Accounts*, Vol. II, 1997, p. 67). Data for the EU and Japan are for 1995, those for the USA for 1994.

[2] Market demand is measured by apparent consumption (production plus imports minus exports). Demand growth has been lower in the USA and highest in Japan, but the data are derived indirectly via information on production and trade, which may not be fully comparable.

Table 5.1: Sectoral growth 1989 to 1996

	EU			Japan			USA			Total		
	Market demand	Value added	Employ-ment	Market demand	Value added	Employ-ment	Market demand	Value added	Employ-ment	Market demand	Value added	Employ-ment
	Growth p.a.											
Food & Beverages	3.0	3.9	-0.5	4.4	2.7	0.7	0.4	3.2	0.3	2.5	3.3	0.0
Tobacco	2.8	14.1	-3.8	5.6	9.2	-4.8	0.0	1.6	-3.7	2.8	5.6	-3.8
Textiles	-0.5	-0.3	-4.5	-0.7	-2.1	-4.7	0.1	0.8	-0.4	-0.4	-0.4	-3.3
Clothing	2.4	0.4	-3.3	3.0	-1.4	-4.5	0.9	-0.6	-3.9	1.8	-0.4	-3.7
Leather Products	1.7	0.6	-3.4	2.5	-2.0	-4.5	0.4	-3.3	-6.3	1.5	-0.9	-4.1
Wood & Products	1.8	1.7	-1.9	3.6	1.3	-1.8	3.2	3.5	0.8	2.8	2.4	-0.8
Pulp, Paper & Products	1.2	2.1	-2.4	4.5	2.6	-1.2	1.9	-0.1	-0.3	2.2	1.1	-1.3
Publishing, Printing	3.2	3.1	-0.9	6.6	4.2	0.0	0.5	2.0	-0.1	3.0	2.8	-0.3
Refined Petroleum	6.1	15.1	-0.8	6.1	14.7	0.2	-3.0	2.4	-2.0	2.8	9.7	-1.1
Chemicals	2.3	2.6	-1.8	5.0	3.3	-0.2	2.1	3.0	-0.9	2.8	3.0	-1.3
Ruber & Plastic Products	3.8	4.3	-0.4	5.8	4.4	0.1	3.0	4.4	1.7	4.1	4.4	0.4
Non-metalic Mineral Products	1.9	1.7	-2.5	4.4	2.0	-1.4	-0.1	1.2	-0.9	2.2	1.7	-1.9
Basic Metals	-1.7	-2.4	-4.8	-0.2	-1.9	-2.4	-0.3	1.3	-1.2	-0.8	-1.0	-3.3
Fabricated Metal	3.0	3.2	-1.1	4.3	2.3	-0.4	1.0	2.6	0.3	2.7	2.7	-0.5
Machinery, Other Fab. Metal	1.6	2.8	-1.9	3.9	2.7	-1.3	1.3	2.9	0.1	2.2	2.8	-1.1
Office Machinery	2.3	-1.3	-3.3	6.6	0.0	-1.5	7.7	4.9	-2.9	5.5	1.8	-2.6
Electrical Machinery	2.9	2.5	-2.4	3.8	3.8	-2.0	0.7	2.0	-0.9	2.6	2.7	-1.9
Radio, TV & Communication	3.7	4.1	-2.1	6.1	5.1	-2.0	6.6	8.6	1.1	5.7	6.3	-1.0
Precision Instruments	1.9	2.7	-2.7	1.7	-0.1	-2.8	0.3	1.3	-2.6	1.1	1.4	-2.7
Motor Vehicles	3.4	2.9	-1.7	5.6	2.6	-0.3	2.0	2.8	1.7	3.5	2.8	-0.5
Other Transport	0.3	1.0	-3.0	4.3	3.7	-0.6	-3.8	-3.3	-5.6	-0.6	-1.1	-4.1
Other Manufacturing	3.6	2.7	-0.2	2.0	-0.8	-2.2	1.4	1.7	0.0	2.3	1.5	-0.4
Total Manufacturing	2.4	2.7	-1.9	4.3	2.5	-1.3	1.3	2.4	-0.5	2.5	2.5	-1.4

Radio, TV & communication: WIFO estimates for EU 1989 to 1992; Japan, USA: data for 1996 WIFO estimates.
Source: DEBA; WIFO calculations.

The dominant trends in demand are also mirrored by the patterns of growth in value added since 1989, although the global distribution of competitive advantage leads to more marked differences between the three economic areas.

Overall value added increased by 2.5% p.a., in line with market demand with growth in Europe slightly exceeding that in Japan and the USA. The fastest growing sectors in Europe were in traditional industries, such as petroleum products and tobacco, which increased production at double-digit rates. Both industries gained shares in common value added at the expense of the USA. Rubber and plastics followed in third place, but growth was fairly even across the three economic areas. Radio, TV and communication equipment was the only 'high tech' sector within Europe's five fastest growing industries.

The European food industry is an illustrative example of how the introduction of new product variations, marketing, and the focus on specific tastes and needs can change the dynamics and structure of a rather mature market. In the process, the food industry has also contradicted Engel's famous law, which predicts a decreasing share of food consumption in high-income countries. Experiencing the fifth highest growth in value added among EU sectors, growth was higher than in the USA[3] and one percentage point higher than growth in total manufacturing. Consequently, the share of value added and the share in consumption increased between 1989 and 1996. The fact that growth was highest in the heterogeneous subgroup 'other products' indicates the positive effect of product differentiation and innovation, since this category typically includes new and upcoming articles (among these are ready-to-eat foods, frozen foods, low calorie foods and foods for special diets). This heterogeneous subgroup created 2 665 additional jobs, contributing to an industry total of 910 456. Of all individual industries, the food industry therefore provides the second highest number of jobs. Together with meat products, which added 15 114 new jobs, these two industries were among the only nine in Europe, in which employment did not decline.

---

[3] Growth in the foods sector was 3.2% in the USA in nominal and real terms. In Europe, nominal growth in value added was higher (3.9%), although prices increased by 1.3%. In Japan, nominal growth of 2.7% is reduced to 0.6% when price increases are taken into account.

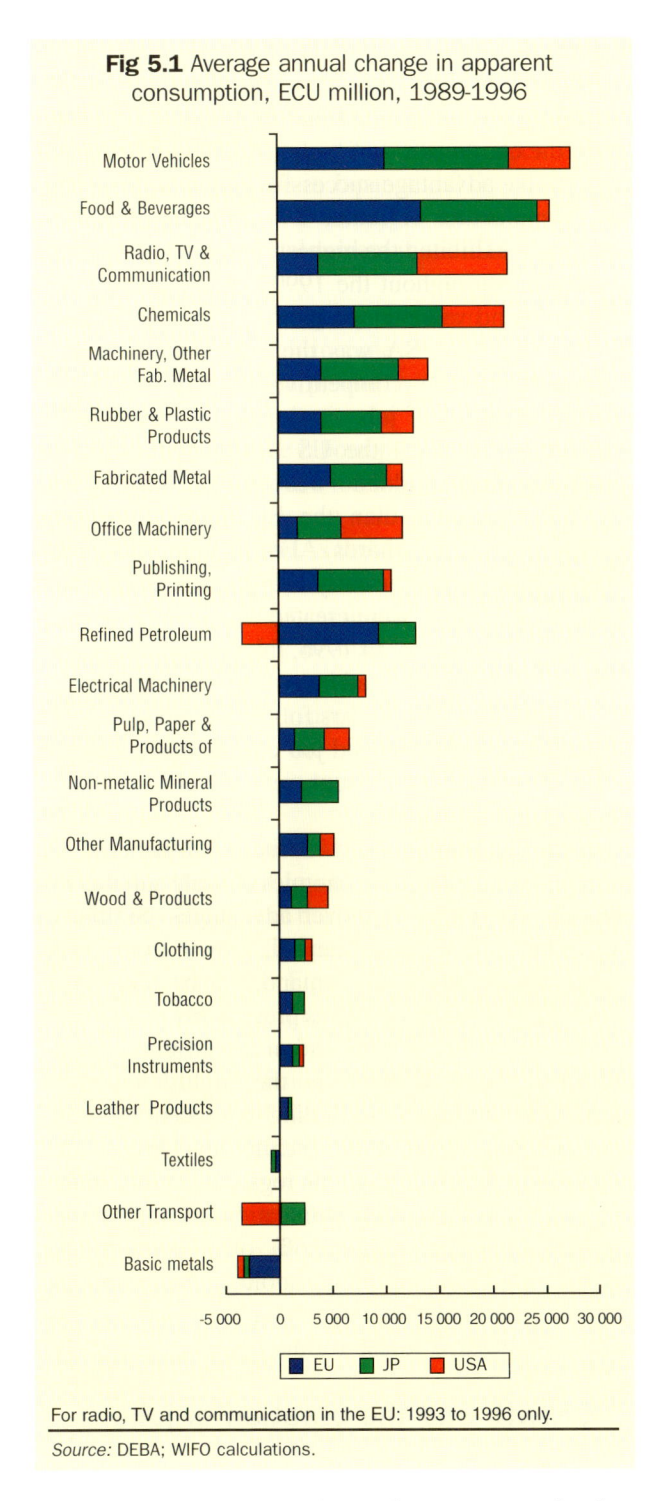

Fig 5.1 Average annual change in apparent consumption, ECU million, 1989-1996

For radio, TV and communication in the EU: 1993 to 1996 only.
Source: DEBA; WIFO calculations.

Petroleum, tobacco, plastic products, communication equipment, and other transport (particularly shipping) are high-growth industries in both Japan and Europe. Radio, TV and communication equipment and office machinery are the two fastest growing industries in the USA.

With regard to employment, the overall pattern again reflects developments in value added. However, in most sectors productivity growth is higher than growth of output, resulting in decreasing employment.

The USA outperformed the EU, as well as Japan: between 1989 and 1996, employment grew in seven out of 22 sectors. Growth was also evident in two Japanese sectors, but no sector in the EU achieved growth in employment.

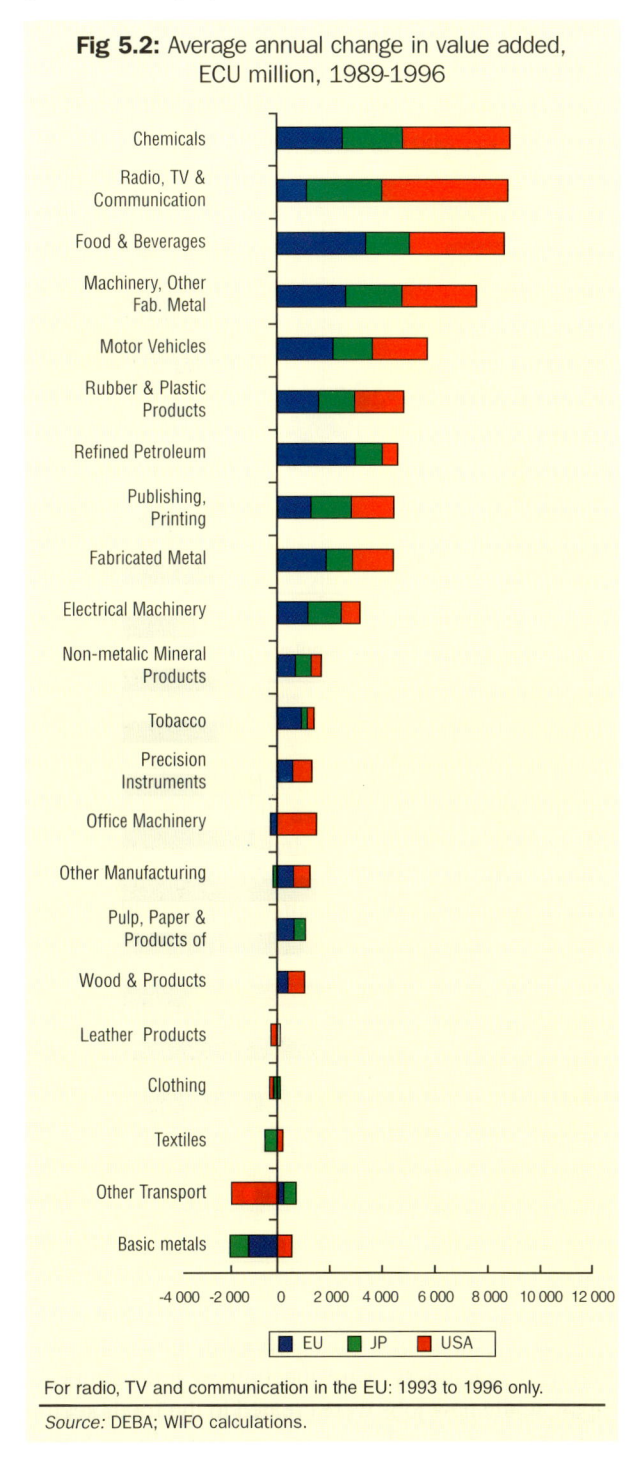

Fig 5.2: Average annual change in value added, ECU million, 1989-1996

For radio, TV and communication in the EU: 1993 to 1996 only.
Source: DEBA; WIFO calculations.

In absolute terms, the EU lost most jobs in machinery, basic metals, and textiles. At the industry level, pharmaceuticals and medical equipment were able to increase employment slightly, both benefiting from the general trend of rising expenditures on health and medical care.

According to the estimations of the model, this requires approximately 7.3% growth in the value added of European manufacturing, compared to 4.4% in Japan and 3.3% in the USA. Figure 5.5 illustrates this point by plotting the relationship between employment growth and output growth as estimated by the panel regression for a typical industry.

Detailed technical information on the data, the results of the estimation, as well as an extension of the basic specifications to include a differentiation across industry types are provided in Chapter 7.

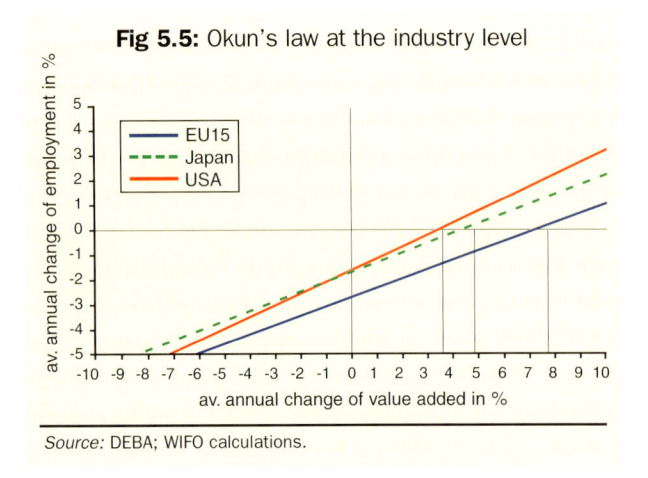

Fig 5.5: Okun's law at the industry level

Source: DEBA; WIFO calculations.

The empirical observation of catching up in labour productivity without significantly higher growth in output adds an important perspective on Europe's unemployment problem. It implies that on average, European manufacturing necessarily loses more jobs per year than Japan or the USA. This loss increases the pressure to create new jobs in the service sector. Furthermore, the evidence suggests that European industries are more eager to rationalise production and substitute capital for labour. This hypothesis should, however, be more deeply investigated in further research.

3. Sectoral development and productivity

Relative to the USA, European manufacturing is catching up in productivity, although productivity levels are still much higher in the USA than in Europe. The following section will analyse to what extent structural developments contribute to aggregate growth in labour productivity.

Productivity is a particularly important measure of competitiveness. When calculated as the ratio of factor inputs to the value of economic output, its attractiveness arises from the fact that it simultaneously reflects two important dimensions of economic performance. The first is the efficiency of production and thus the technological and organisational knowledge employed and the second is the willingness to pay for that output, thus reflecting quality as perceived by consumers and dependent on product development, design and marketing skills. Nevertheless the empirical assessment of productivity exhibits some shortcomings, which require that it be analysed as a complement to and not in place of other indicators such as market shares in foreign trade or flows in foreign direct investment. The first reason is that lack of a reliable database on factor inputs other than labour means that the analysis is usually restricted to labour productivity. The second concern deals with underlying assumptions on market structure: although the value of output is systematically distorted by the type of competitive process dominating the market place, any direct comparison between countries inevitably neglects differences in the market structures of distinct economic areas. In addition, it must be remembered that productivity growth is highly variable when measured over short periods of time because of its sensitivity to the business cycle. During periods of high growth in value added, for example at the beginning of an upward movement, high rates of productivity growth are typical concomitants.

Keeping in mind the limitations mentioned above, two questions will be addressed in the following analysis: Whether and to what extent does the sectoral composition of manufacturing output affect (i) differences in overall productivity between countries, or (ii) changes in total productivity over time?
Decomposition techniques, as recently demonstrated by Davies-Lyons (1991, 1996)[5] and Dollar-Wolff (1995)[6], offer a particularly instructive approach. The basic idea is to compare actual productivity levels of total manufacturing in individual countries with a hypothetical benchmark of aggregate productivity under the assumption of uniform or at least constant size of all industries. Eliminating structural effects, this benchmark isolates the general trends, which apply equally across industries. Contrasting this benchmark to actual labour productivity allows the inference of information about the impact of the structural component.

---

[5] Davies, S., Lyons, B., 'Characterising relative performance: the productivity advantage of foreign owned firms in the UK', *Oxford Economic Papers*, No 43, 1991, pp. 584-595.
Davies, S., Lyons, B., et al., 'Industrial Organisation in the European Union', *Structure, Strategy, and the Competitive Mechanism*, Oxford University Press, Oxford, 1996.

[6] Dollar, D., Wolff, E.N., *Competitiveness, Convergence, and International Specialisation*, MIT Press, Cambridge, MA, 1993.

Structural effects on productivity differentials

The impact of sectoral composition on existing gaps in productivity levels between the individual Member States of the EU, as well as between the EU, Japan and the USA, is identified via the application of a decomposition analysis developed by Davies-Lyons (1991).

Looking at the distinct effects of locational and structural components on differences in productivity levels relative to Japan and the USA in 1995 (see Box 5.1), the EU does not appear to suffer from structural deficits in the sense of being less specialised in high productivity industries. The difference in aggregate labour productivity[7] is entirely due to general locational components, irrespective of the sectoral composition of production (see Table 5.2). The purely locational component, reflecting differences in productivity and assuming uniform distribution of industries of equal size across the EU, Japan and the USA, would even be higher. This implies that the structural component alone would even speak somewhat in favour of European productivity.

Comparing the locational and structural components of the gaps in labour productivity between individual Member States of the EU illustrates that sectoral composition may nevertheless matter. The impact of the structural component differs across Member States. It is strongest in Ireland, Finland, Sweden, and the Netherlands, and also exerts a positive influence in France and to a lesser extent in Germany.[8] In all of these countries, the sectoral composition of production favours a higher level of labour productivity relative to the EU. The current patterns of sectoral specialisation have a slightly negative effect on relative productivity performance in Greece, Denmark, the UK, and Italy, whereas in Spain and Portugal the impact of the structural component is substantial.

Box 5.1: Decomposition of productivity differentials

Following a decomposition technique developed by Davies-Lyons (1991), the ratios of aggregate index numbers are decomposed into two components reflecting relative differences (i) in the distribution of industries and (ii) in performance within individual industries. Multiplication of the two components again gives the true value of the aggregate index.

For the current research, this method is applied to aggregate gaps in labour productivity between pairs of countries or different economic areas. Calculations are restricted to first-tier decomposition, omitting further decomposition of the resulting two components, which are considerably more complex.

The formula for decomposition emerges after rearranging the correlation coefficient (r) between the two variables a and b. The total productivity gap (R) can then be expressed as dependent of the respective arithmetic means of labour productivity (avp_a, avp_b), the correlation coefficients between employment shares and labour productivity ($r^{e,p}_a$, $r^{e,p}_b$), and the coefficients of variation (vc^e_a, vc^e_b; vc^p_a, vc^p_a): R = T x S = (avp_a/avp_b) x (1+ $r^{e,p}_a$ vc^e_a vc^p_a)/(1+ $r^{e,p}_b$ vc^e_b vc^p_b)

The general within industries component T is the ratio of the unweighted means of labour productivity in locations A and B, respectively. The structural component S reveals the impact of differences between A and B on the distribution of industries with lower or higher productivity. The total productivity gap R is the product of both effects.

To give a hypothetical example, if R = T x S = 150.00 = 130.00 x 115.38, then these numbers reveal the following three facts:
i) Total labour productivity in location A is 50% higher than in location B.
ii) If in both locations employment were identically and uniformly distributed across industries, the aggregate differential would fall to 30%.
iii) Even if average productivity across industries were identical in both locations, the larger shares of high productivity industries in location A would be capable of generating a productivity lead of approximately 15% on their own.

---

[7] Both Japan and the USA achieved considerably higher labour productivity in manufacturing measured at current prices than the EU total. Yet the absolute size of this gap must be interpreted with care. The comparison of absolute levels of labour productivity suffers from severe shortcomings stemming e.g. from exchange rate regimes, the influence of PPPs, as well as the lack of information on actual working hours per employee.

[8] For both Germany and France, the structural component is more pronounced when measured at the sectoral level.

Chapter 6
European industries in world markets

In this chapter, stylised facts will be used to illustrate how European industries have performed on world markets compared to their counterparts in Japan and the USA, and how their performance has changed over time. The analysis focuses on external performance, taking into account the results on internal performance from the preceding chapter. Specifically, the analysis investigates the EU's strategy for coping with the competition of low wage countries by shifting to higher quality and more sophisticated segments in markets with differentiated products.

Competitiveness has been defined as the ability of an economy to increase its standard of living and to create employment, while maintaining a sustainable external balance. Internal and external performance are strongly linked: in open economies, growth in output and the creation of jobs requires industries to be competitive on an international scale. Otherwise, imports would increase, thereby dampening the prospects for job creation in domestic firms. High and increasing productivity is therefore the precondition for exports and domestic production.

There are at least three reasons for a specific focus on external performance. Firstly, trade balances and international market shares are very sensitive indicators of changes in competitive position. Compared to domestic production, which is often distorted by local demand conditions, trade data provide relatively early signals of shifts in the balance of competitive strengths and weaknesses. Secondly, the external analysis profits from the fact that trade statistics are less blurred by national conventions and accounting systems, and are available at a very disaggregated level. Finally, trade statistics permit concentration on the qualitative element of competitiveness, revealing for example whether low prices or high quality determines the competitive edge, or whether a country is specialising in the high or low quality segment of a market. Additionally, economic theories differ to some extent in their forecasts on specialisation and performance.

1. Market shares and trade balances

Favourable European trade performance

The overall assessment of external trade performance for the EU appears rather favourable: European manufacturing exports are greater than those of Japan and the USA, even when intra-European trade is excluded. Market shares are stable; the trade balance is positive and increasing.

While shares in the world market decreased both in Japan (from 19.2% to 14.5%) and the USA (from 20.2% to 18.8%), the EU market share remained stable at approximately 27% (see Table 6.1). At the same time, increasing market shares were achieved by dynamic Asian economies (from 15.1% to 21.0%) and by countries in transition. In absolute numbers, the EU increased its trade surplus from ECU 28 billion in 1989 to ECU 130 billion in 1996, while Japan's surplus fell below the EU level (ECU 107 billion) and the USA accrued a deficit of ECU 146 billion.

Table 6.1: Trade in total manufacturing

	Market shares 1989	1996	Trade balance 1989 1000 mill. ECU	1996	Exports Annual growth in %	Imports
EU	27.0	26.9	28.1	130.2	7.9	5.3
Japan	19.2	14.5	121.7	107.4	3.7	7.8
USA	20.2	18.8	-125.1	-146.4	6.8	5.5
'Other countries'	35.4	42.0	-1.9	-123.3	9.2	11.3
Among them: DYNAS	15.1	21.0	22.0	-100.4	13.1	18.4

Shares in world market: Exports as a percentage of world imports.
DYNAS is a subcategory of "Other Countries": Thailand, Indonesia, Malaysia, Singapore, Philippines, China, South-Korea, Taiwan, Hong Kong.

The sum of market shares is more than 100%, due to differences in the reporting behaviour of countries. In some cases the countries of origin report their exports, but the destination countries do not report all their imports for example, for confidentiality reasons. One illustrative example is arms and ammunition.

Source: COMPET; WIFO calculations.

CHAPTER 6

Table 6.2: Top performing sectors and industries according to their share in world market

Top market shares 1996		Top winners: increase in market share		
EU	Share 1996 in %	EU	Change 1996/89	Share 1996 in %
Top 3 sectors		**Top 3 sectors**		
Other transport equipment	49.1	Other transport equipment	14.5	49.1
Machinery and equipment n. e. c.	45.5	Motor vehicles, trailers and semi-trailers	5.9	29.8
Other non-metallic mineral products	43.4	Coke, refined petroleum and nuclear fuel	4.4	19.0
Top 5 industries		**Top 5 industries**		
Steam generators	111.3	Steam generators	47.2	111.3
Ceramic tiles and flags	95.4	and ammunition	38.0	55.0
"Dairy products; ice cream"	89.6	Ships and boats	32.0	67.1
Beverages	73.6	Aircraft and spacecraft	16.0	53.0
Tanks, reservoirs, central heating radiators, boilers	71.2	TV, radio transmitters, apparatus for line telephony	10.5	34.4
Japan		**Japan**		
Top 3 sectors		**Top 3 sectors**		
Motor vehicles, trailers and semi-trailers	31.1	Other transport equipment	4.3	17.7
Machinery and equipment n. e. c.	22.2	Coke, refined petroleum and nuclear fuel	1.7	2.5
Radio, TV and communication equipment	21.6	Tobacco products	0.4	3.3
Top 5 industries		**Top 5 industries**		
Ships and boats	73.4	Ships and boats	33.1	73.4
Motorcycles and bicycles	46.9	Cement, lime and plaster	3.8	18.3
Accumulators, primary cells, primary batteries	33.0	Parts and accessories for motor vehicles	3.1	31.3
Optical instruments, photographic equipment	31.9	Refined petroleum products	2.1	2.3
Motor vehicles	31.6	Bricks, tiles and construction products	1.2	5.3
USA		**USA**		
Top 3 sectors		**Top 3 sectors**		
Tobacco products	71.2	Motor vehicles, trailers and semi-trailers	4.2	22.5
Other transport equipment	43.0	Fabricated metal products	3.4	18.9
Publishing, printing, reproduction	35.6	Rubber and plastic products	2.8	21.4
Top 5 industries		**Top 5 industries**		
Weapons and ammunition	144.5	Weapons and ammunition	9.7	144.4
Tobacco products	71.2	Meat products	7.9	32.9
Aircraft and spacecraft	58.0	Parts, accessories for motor vehicles	7.4	40.1
Grain mill products and starches	44.4	TV, radio transmitters, apparatus for line telephony	6.2	23.1
Medical equipment	41.7	Other fabricated metal products	6.1	19.4

Market share: Exports as a percentage of world imports. They do not add up e.g. due to divergent methods of reporting.

Source: COMPET, WIFO calculations

Europe's highest export market shares appear in sectors with medium technical sophistication. Three metal-based sectors (other transport, machinery, and fabricated metal) are complemented by mineral products and the chemical sector in the top five, ranked according to market shares in 1996 (see Table 6.2). The machinery, transport and metal sector includes 8 of the 10 industries with the highest gains in market shares. The large increases achieved by aircraft and spacecraft and TV and radio transmitters as well as by steam generators and weapons and ammunitions hint at some EU inroads in technically more sophisticated industries. As far as the trade balance is concerned, machinery plus motor vehicles together create a surplus of ECU 100 billion, and the chemical industry adds another ECU 32 billion.

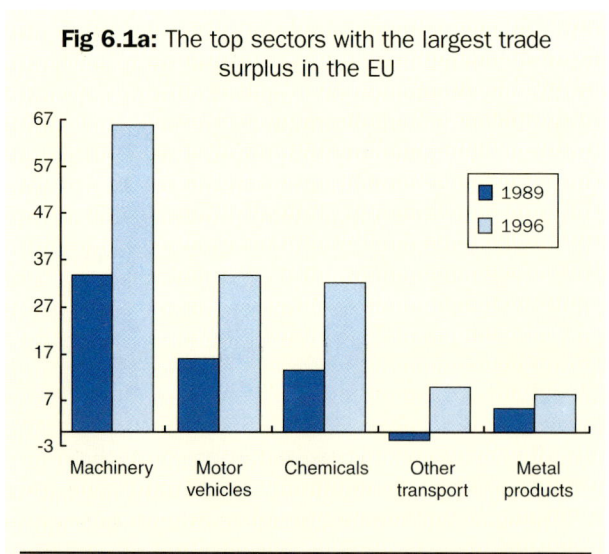

Fig 6.1a: The top sectors with the largest trade surplus in the EU

Source: COMPET; WIFO calculations.

Fig 6.1b: The top sectors with the largest trade surplus in Japan

[Bar chart showing 1989 and 1996 data for: Vehicles, Machinery, Radio TV, Elect. Machinery, Computer]

Source: COMPET; WIFO calculations.

Fig 6.1c: The top sectors with the largest trade surplus in the USA

[Bar chart showing 1989 and 1996 data for: Other transport, Chemicals, Machinery, Instruments, Tobacco]

Source: COMPET; WIFO calculations.

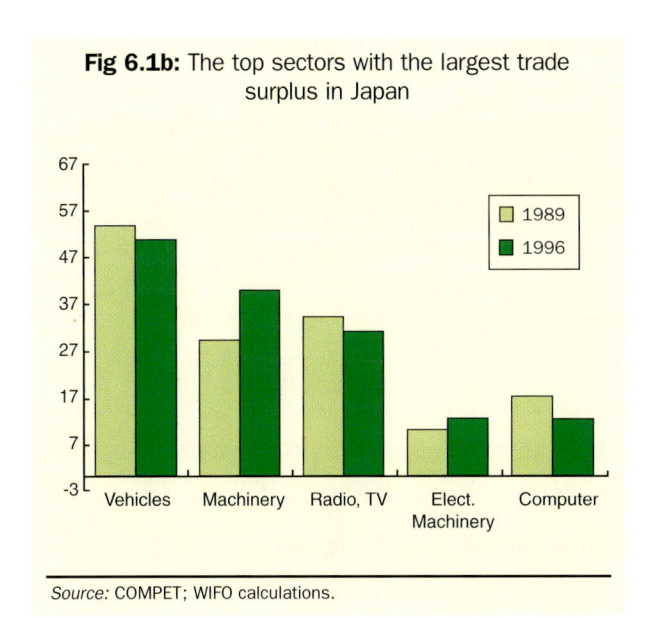

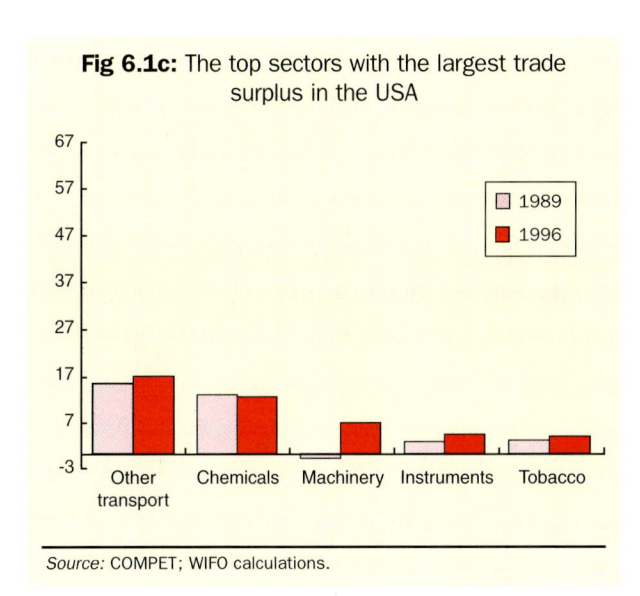

The USA quickly goes multinational

By far the greatest market share held by the USA is in the tobacco industry, followed by other transport equipment (for example aircraft and spacecraft). The USA also enjoys a strong position in printing, paper products and precision instruments. Disaggregation to industry level reveals a two-tiered picture: some of the leading industries are resource based, partly linked to the food sector (tobacco, mill products, meat), while others are primarily technology based (aircraft and spacecraft, medical equipment, precision instruments). The largest gains in market shares have been achieved in the vehicles industry (without decreasing the absolute deficit of ECU 46 billion), in metal products and rubber and plastics. In all of these sectors, gains were made at the expense of Japan and not of Europe. In nine of the ten sectors in which the USA gained large market shares, Japan's share was reduced.

Box 6.1: Three European success stories in fast growing industries

The pharmaceutical industry is a high tech industry with fast growth, high research and great emphasis on quality and goodwill. At 56%, Europe's world market share in manufacturing is much larger than that of the USA or Japan. Both are suffering from decreasing market shares and negative trade balances. However, in absolute size of value added, US production is the largest. In both the USA and Japan, the share of pharmaceuticals in total manufacturing value added is larger than in the EU. Market growth for the total of the three economic areas is 7% p.a.. European manufacturing increased nominal value added by 7.5%; prices increased by roughly 1%. Employment increased by 14 100 and today amounts to 440 000 persons.

Medical equipment increased its value added in Europe by 7.6%, p.a., while market growth in the combined area EU-Japan-USA was 5.3%. The USA has the highest market share, and produces two thirds of the value added of this market. This indicates further growth potential for Europe. Europe's trade balance is slightly positive, but below the US level. Employment increased in Europe by 11 400 (+1% p.a.) and is now 173 000.

The production of railway vehicles is growing by 7.4% p.a. in Europe. This rate is much higher than in the USA and Japan, as is this industry's share in value added. Europe's world market share is approaching 50%, the trade balance is positive, although trade is not considerable. Employment is decreasing slightly, but less than in total manufacturing. Additionally, there is a large potential for complementary service jobs, especially in the planning of systems, the supply of components and the maintenance of tracks.

The data indicate that the USA does not attempt to exploit comparative advantages to the same extent as Europe or Japan via the trade of products. The three largest contributors to the trade balance at the sectoral level add up to ECU 38 billion only for the USA, ECU 132 billion for Europe and ECU 122 billion for Japan (see Fig. 6.1). At the industry level, the same tendency holds: no large surpluses are accrued, and existing ones tend to evaporate, rather than accumulate over time. One probable explanation is that US firms exploit advantages earlier via direct investment abroad, while European and Japanese firms prefer to exploit competitive advantages (longer) through trade. This may partly be due to a stronger emphasis in the USA on firm specific advantages (for example by innovation and marketing)

Box 6.2: The data

The DEBA database is used for internal performance. This database provides consistent data for value added, employment, as well as other main indicators for EU countries, Japan and the USA. Data are fairly complete from 1989 to 1996. In some 3-digit industries, estimates for missing data primarily up to 1993 and for 1996 are provided. Nominal value added at factor costs has been selected as the main activity indicator.

The analysis of external performance is based on the COMPET database, which consists of exports and imports for each of 59 reporting countries. The 'world market' is defined according to world imports, taken from the sum of all imports of the available reporting countries. These comprise more than 90% of total world trade. Intra-European trade is excluded throughout the report. Missing are mainly developing countries and some countries in transition. The 'market share' is defined as the ratio of an economy's exports to the 'world market'. This 'export of a country to the import of the world' market share concept is chosen since it is closest to the economic concept of a firm's share in the total sales of a market.

The following acronyms are used: CEEC (transition economies, including the Czech Republic, Bulgaria, Estonia, Hungary, Latvia, Lithuania, Poland, Romania, Slovakia, Slovenia); DYNAS (dynamic Asian economies including China: Thailand, Indonesia, Malaysia, Singapore, Philippines, China, South Korea, Taiwan, Hong Kong).

Additionally, information on qualitative performance is based on the COMEXT database, which provides disaggregated data for up to 6-digit product groups and allows for more detailed information on the EU trade structure. Trade data from COMEXT are linked to the NACE industry classification by a correspondence table for 1996.

Throughout the study, 2-digit data are referred to as sectors and 3-digit data as industries (officially, EUROSTAT labels them 'divisions' and 'groups').

---

in contrast to the general comparative advantages of a particular location (for example factor prices, market access or available skills). This question will be further investigated in the following chapter. In any case, going multinational rapidly implies limits on the extent of trade surpluses in sectors with firm specific assets. Income in production and for blue-collar workers is reduced, whereas income from capital and financial assets increases.

Japan focuses on comparative advantages

Japanese exports are heavily concentrated, notably in engineering skills. Indeed, all sectors in which Japan has high market shares are skill-intensive industries. Motor vehicles and machinery lead the sector ranking, radio, TV and communication equipment, electrical machinery, precision instruments and other transport equipment follow. At industry level, all but one of the top ten are engineering industries encompassing ships and boats, motorcycles and motor vehicles, as well as accumulators and optical instruments. The top 4 sectors cover 60% of overall Japanese exports, compared with 48% in Europe and 47% in the USA (see Table 6.3). Switching to the industry level, 62% of Japanese exports stem from the 10 largest exporting industries, again compared to 51% in the USA and only 42% in Europe. With respect to imports, there is no significant difference in these quasi-concentration rates across the three areas, which indicates that specialisation and not differences in demand are the driving force.

Table 6.3: Concentration of exports in the EU, Japan and the USA 1996

	EU	Japan	USA
Share of 4 largest sectors			
Exports	47.6	60.3	46.6
Imports	39.4	34.0	41.6
Share of 10 largest industries			
Exports	42.4	62.2	51.0
Imports	32.1	39.5	42.0
Trade surplus of 4 largest sectors	141,409	134,393	42,756
10 industries with largest disadvantage			
Standard deviation of RCA across industries	0.557	1.825	1.002
Import/export relation (RCA)	-1.576	-5.395	-2.225
Import/value added share	177.9	89.9	276.1
Export/value added share	66.1	0.8	26.3
Trade deficit	-49.3	-26.6	-35.8

RCA: Revealed comparative advantage $\ln((X_i/M_i)/(X/M))$

Source: DEBA, COMEXT, COMPET; WIFO calculations.

The high negative specialisation ratios exhibited by Japan as soon as comparative disadvantages are revealed in any particular industry are unrivalled.

The average of the industries with the greatest de-specialisation (measured by the lowest ten RCA values) is -5.4 in Japan, compared to -1.6 in Europe and -2.2 in the USA (see Fig. 6.2). Exports as a share of value added in these industries is 66% in Europe, 26% in the USA, but only 1% in Japan. This indicates that Japan gives up exports completely, while in Europe and in the USA some firms continue supplying in niches. However, imports do not rise so much in Japan, amounting to ECU 27 billion (ECU 78 billion in the EU and ECU 40 billion in the USA). The relation between imports and domestic value added is 178% in Europe, 276% in the USA, and only 90% in Japan. This implies that production for the home market continues to a certain extent, indicating either consumer preferences for domestic varieties or some sort of import barrier.

The extremely favourable starting point in 1989 explains why in Japan almost no sector has been able to expand its share in the world market. Increases in individual industries were moderate; some of them were in construction materials and in the chemical sector and only two in sophisticated industries. In the ten industries in which Japan gained market shares, the USA was confronted with losses in eight, Europe in seven.

Large inroads for emerging economies

The highest amount of other market shares of countries outside EU-Japan-USA is in textiles and wood processing, clothing apparel and tobacco. Their market shares in world exports increased from 35.4% to 42.0% - mainly driven by the dynamics of emerging Asian countries, which for example managed to raise their shares in office machinery (20.3% in 1989 to 35.2% in 1996).

The significant inroads of countries outside EU-Japan-USA in market shares have to be put into perspective by also examining the dynamics of imports. In trade with the EU, these countries have a deficit of ECU 135 billion. This implies that the success of new competitors may reduce employment opportunities in some European industries, but Europe is increasing its exports even faster, so that globalisation cannot easily be scorned as a source of net losses in employment. The only country group - disregarding Japan - that enjoys a surplus in trade with the EU, are the dynamic Asian countries, with which the EU's deficit in 1996 amounted to ECU 7 billion.

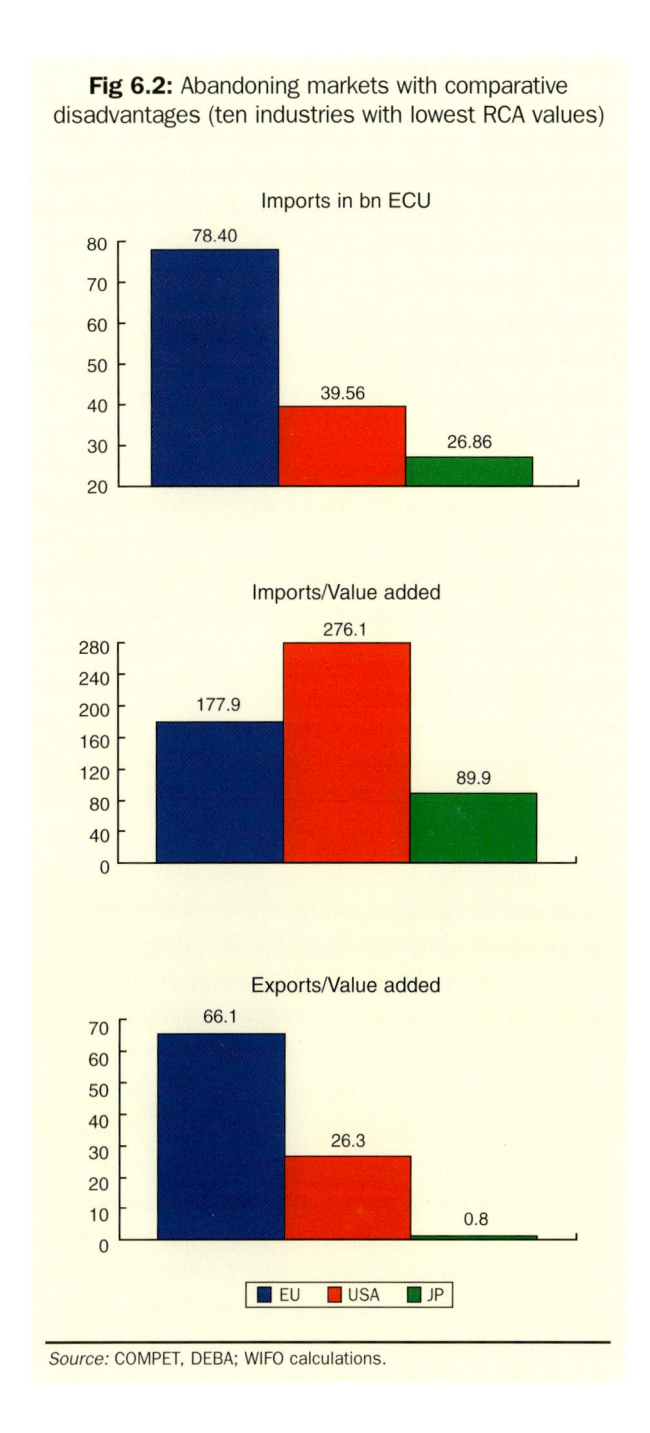

Fig 6.2: Abandoning markets with comparative disadvantages (ten industries with lowest RCA values)

Imports in bn ECU
- EU: 78.40
- USA: 39.56
- JP: 26.86

Imports/Value added
- EU: 177.9
- USA: 276.1
- JP: 89.9

Exports/Value added
- EU: 66.1
- USA: 26.3
- JP: 0.8

Source: COMPET, DEBA; WIFO calculations.

2. Competition in quality

Rationale and measurement

The more an economy is able to produce goods which are appreciated for their quality and for fulfilling specific needs, the larger the potential for further increases in living standards, and the smaller the overall exposure to low cost producers. A high wage area facing new competitors has to differentiate products and shift into higher priced segments or into less price sensitive industries.

The unit values of exports and imports will be compared to reveal whether the EU successfully specialises in higher valued market segments. Further disaggregation indicates for which exports the price or the quality defines the prime competitive edge. Finally, industries are classified according to their respective price elasticities and the importance of quality competition. Producing higher quality and increasing productivity may be alternative or complementary strategies. Both strategies imply creating more value for a given quantity. Productivity is usually thought of as the relation of a physical output to a measure of labour input (labour productivity) or to a weighted input of several quantitatively measured inputs (total factor productivity). One way to measure quality is to estimate the value created for the consumer by the consumption of one unit of a good. Thus productivity stresses the relation between a physical output and a

---

Box 6.3: Unit values and their use

The unit value is defined as nominal value divided into physical volume. Increasing unit values may either be due to rising demand or rising costs. But unit values also reflect changes in quality, shifts to higher product segments and to more specific value enhancing features. Therefore, unit value is often applied as an indicator in attempts to measure quality and vertical product differentiation.

However, its use has been limited by the fact that high quality and high costs caused by less efficient techniques are difficult to disentangle. Aiginger (1997)[a] shows that the unit value is near to a productivity measure, if the product is homogenous and the number of workers needed to produce one unit of output is relatively constant. But the unit value approaches a pure price or consumer valuation if the product or service is differentiated and the value is related to the input unit (counselling fee per hour, construction fee per square meter or per kilo cement).

The hierarchy of unit values across industries also reflects the number of stages in processing. In some cases, it is of limited value, since there are industries in which the unit values are intrinsically higher than in others, while neither high tech, nor skilled labour, nor physical capital is involved. This holds for example for textile and apparel industries in which the unit values are high, since the weight in tons is low. The same holds for precious metals, where supply is scarce relative to demand. Therefore, jewellery, leather, furs, footwear and apparel are among the top industries as far as the absolute unit value is concerned, without indicating for example the use of skilled labour or research. High tech or high skill industries - like aircraft and spacecraft, watches and clocks, TV and radio transmitters and instruments - are also among the industries with the highest export unit values. In all these industries, unit values are much higher for processed goods and those made with large inputs of research and human capital, than for semi-finished goods, structural metals etc. At the bottom of a list ranking industries according to their unit values are industries at the early stages of processing, producing inputs for other industries, such as cement, bricks, coke oven products, petroleum, saw milling, or planing and impregnation of wood. At sectoral level, the ranking of unit values fits reasonably well into the notion of competition in product quality: the four sectors at the top of absolute unit values in the EU are four technically sophisticated industries: precision instruments, office machinery, TV and communication equipment and other transport equipment. The four sectors with the lowest export unit values are basic goods industries (refined petroleum, construction materials, basic metals, pulp and paper).

Additionally, it has been shown that at national level, countries with higher incomes tend to export goods with high unit values and import those with low unit values.

Comparing the hierarchy of industries according to both unit values and labour productivity reveals similarities and differences between the two concepts. The main coincidence lies in the high tech industries mentioned above, which enjoy high unit values and high labour productivity. Among the exceptions is the evaluation of medical instruments and other transport as industries with low labour productivity but high unit values. The second difference lies in the evaluation of capital- and energy-intensive basic goods industries. Petroleum, paper and basic metals are highly ranked by labour productivity, but have low unit values. The third group consists of textiles and clothing industries, which have low labour productivity but intrinsically high unit values.

[a] Aiginger, K., 'The use of unit values to discriminate between price and quality competition', Cambridge *Journal of Economics*, Vol. 21, 1997, pp. 571-592.

Table 6.4: Quality premium of EU exports over imports 1996

	Exports	Imports	Export unit value	Import unit value	Relative unit value	Higher export unit value of EU	
	1000 mill. ECU		ECU/kg			Number of	
						Sectors	Industries
Total trade of EU	575.6	452.0	2.070	1.492	1.387	17	71
EU trade vs. USA	104.1	96.2	2.736	2.616	1.046	11	49
EU trade vs. Japan	33.3	51.4	6.177	12.245	0.504	11	42
EU trade vs. "Other Countries"	438.3	304.4	1.869	1.162	1.609	20	77
EU trade vs. DYNAS	85.4	91.5	3.246	3.820	0.850	17	70

Relative unit value = Unit value export/unit value import (=Quality premium)
DYNAS: Thailand, Indonesia, Malaysia, Singapore, Philippines, China, South-Korea, Taiwan, Hong Kong.
Total number of sectors n=22; total number of industries n=95.

Source: COMPET; WIFO calculations.

physical input, while quality emphasises value per output. An increase in value added per employee, however, is a measure that should ideally include changes in values as well as productivity increases, in the sense defined above. It is interesting to see which component prevails: that of physical output to physical inputs or that of shifting to higher valued goods.

Quality premium in total trade

The export unit value of European manufacturing is 40% higher than that of imports (see Table 6.4). Roughly half of this 'quality mark up' in European trade comes from specialisation in high unit value industries, and roughly half from higher unit values within the same industries. If exports had the same (quantitative) composition as imports, the unit values would still be 20% higher than that of aggregate imports. This 'within industry' premium of higher unit values in exports than imports applies to 18 sectors out of 22, and 71 industries out of 95.

The industries in which Europe has higher unit values in exports than in imports can be broadly split into two groups.

- Firstly, industries in which the EU is a net importer and low cost countries have positive specialisation. Consequently, the export unit values are much higher for the EU, since it concentrates only on the highest valued market segments. This group comprises leather clothes, textile weaving, as well as sports goods and furniture.

- Secondly, technically sophisticated industries with differentiated products, in which Europe faces tough competition from suppliers in Japan and the USA. In most of these industries, the unit values of exports are higher than of imports, but due to competition within the industrialised counties, the ratio is lower than in the industries mentioned above. Examples are audio-visual apparatus, office machinery, and optical instruments.

Unit values of European exports are lower than for imports in 24 industries. The largest are non-ferrous metals, saw milling, certain industries in the food sector, and also some electrical industries. Basic metals is the only sector in which import unit values are significantly higher. In the industries labelled other transports, a large negative margin between the export unit value and the import unit value declined considerably.

Quality premium in trade with Japan and the USA

Unit values are not available for Japanese and US exports, since some industries do not report quantities consistent with European data. The following analysis is therefore restricted to bilateral trade flows, taking the EU as the reporting country.

European trade with the USA is approximately balanced. European exports to the USA are 7% higher than imports and the unit value of European exports is 5% higher than that of the imports from the USA. These margins apply relatively evenly across industries and sectors. Significantly higher unit values, which are to the advantage of the EU, are given for the food sector, in which European exports exceed imports by 57% and cover higher priced segments within 7 out of 9 industries. Similar specialisation is revealed in the leather industries and in wood processing. Within the larger industries, the unit value is 46% higher in the vehicles industry. It is somewhat higher in the chemical sector and lower in the machinery sector. In several sophisticated industries, such as office machinery, electronic components and special purpose machinery, the EU exports goods at a lower unit value to the USA than it imports. Pharmaceuticals, aircraft and spacecraft are examples in which Europe has higher unit values.

European exports to Japan cover only 65% of imports. The total trade deficit in manufacturing can be explained by the lower unit values of European exports. While the unit value of European imports is 12.2 ECU/kg, its exports are priced at only 6.2 ECU/kg. This significant effect does not stem from differences within industries - the numbers of sectors and industries with higher and lower unit values are roughly equal - but rather from Japan's concentration on higher valued goods (engineering and electronic industries), while the exports of labour and resource intensive industries are largely abandoned. In the vehicle industry, European exports are valued 70% higher in bilateral trade. In office machinery, the European unit value of exports is nearly four times higher than that of imports. Similar relations are evident in the apparel industry and TV and radio equipment. In resource based industries, Japan's trade is balanced, but focuses on higher priced segments.

Surplus and quality versus other areas

Europe's trade surplus stems from trade with countries outside the EU-Japan-USA-area: exports of ECU 440 billion compared with imports of only ECU 300 billion, resulting in a surplus larger than the total surplus. The unit values are lower than those for total trade on both sides, the export unit value is 1.9 ECU/kg and the import value is only 1.2 ECU/kg. The quality premium amounts to 60%, and reflects differences both in endowments and in vertical product differentiation. Large differences are exhibited within the 'other countries'. While the unit values of exports in the EU's trade with Central and Eastern European transition countries are much higher than for imports, they are slightly lower in trade with dynamic Asian economies. As with trade with Japan, this stems mainly from the high specialisation of the dynamic Asian countries in the engineering and electronic industries. However, there is a difference between Japan and the other dynamic Asian countries insofar as the latter produce at lower prices (two thirds of the exports from these countries are lower valued than European exports). This pattern reflects the strategic focus of domestic as well as multinational enterprises (partly Japanese and European) on labour intensive production processes within technically sophisticated and dynamically growing industries. This strategy permits the dynamic Asian countries to benefit simultaneously from a powerful combination of general locational advantages (low wages) on the one hand, and firm specific advantages (based on technological knowledge) on the other.

The major findings may be summarised as follows: the total European trade surplus originates in a general quality mark up and this quality mark up stems from trade with countries other than Japan and the USA.

Competition within the industrialised countries is an important benchmark, specifically for the high valued segment of the market, which may provide a valuable early indication of future developments in quality competition. But in quantitative terms, the largest part of total European trade flows stems from the exchange of goods with countries other than Japan and the USA. To give a few examples: of the total exports from the EU, only 18% go to the USA and 6% to Japan. 10.1% of the EU's exports go to the Central and Eastern European transition economies and 14.5% to the dynamic Asian countries. The respective shares as source of the EU's imports are 8.2% and 16.9%. Two western European countries, which are not members of the Union (Switzerland and Norway), account for a larger part of the EU's total trade than Japan. However, these figures should not downplay the importance of the competitive performance between the EU, Japan and the USA, especially since all of them also compete for export shares in other markets.

Four segments of competition according to quality and price

Information regarding relative prices and physical quantities traded is used to reveal whether the EU trades more in industries with a high price elasticity or in industries in which competition in quality dominates. Other things being equal, demand is negatively related to price. Consequently, this implies that if an economy is able to sell products at higher unit values and, nevertheless, enjoys an export surplus, there is a supply of higher quality within the same industry. In the following analysis, this rationale is used to assess the quality position of the EU and to rank industries according to their respective price elasticities.

- Successful quality competition: In 36 industries, the EU is a net exporter in quantity, despite higher unit values. This sector contains mainly technically demanding engineering industries. The largest surplus occurs in other special purpose machinery and in motor vehicles; considerable surpluses also occur in pharmaceuticals, machinery for producing mechanical power as well as air- and spacecraft. The total surplus generated in this market segment is ECU 161 billion. 51% of total European exports originate in this segment. The common surplus is larger than in total trade.

- Structural problem area: Another segment, in which prices and net quantities have the same sign, is labelled 'structural problem area', since the EU exhibits both a deficit in trade and lower unit values. This group contains only 7 industries. Other apparel is creating the largest deficit, followed by basic precious and non-ferrous metals. Electronic components, fish and fish products, saw milling, planing and impregnation of wood, man-made fibres and the processing of nuclear fuel are the other industries in which unit values are high, but quantities exported are smaller than those imported. Imports are worth ECU 83 billion (18% of total imports), and the trade deficit amounts to ECU 46 billion.

- Gap in price competitiveness: The EU suffers a trade deficit in terms of physical quantities in 35 industries, while its unit values are higher in exports than in imports. Basic chemicals, petroleum products, pulp and paper, textile weaving and furniture belong to this segment. The single largest deficit occurs in the office machinery and computer industry, where the EU has a deficit in the low and medium ranged quality segments. The EU exports only in the higher valued niches of the market. As a consequence, the unit value of exports is 50% above that of imports, although in physical quantities exports are low. The total group of industries in which unit values are higher in European exports than in imports, but the quantities sold are lower, comprises imports of ECU 174 billion. Taken together, the overall trade deficit only amounts to ECU 27 billion.

- Successful price competition: In this group, the EU has lower prices (in terms of the ratio of unit values in export to imports) and simultaneously enjoys a trade surplus when measured in physical quantities. This segment comprises 17 rather small industries, ranging from other chemicals or machine tools to detergents. The exports of all industries together generate ECU 98 billion or 17% of total exports. The trade surplus is ECU 35 billion, which is considerably below the ECU 161 billion in the segment of successful quality competition.

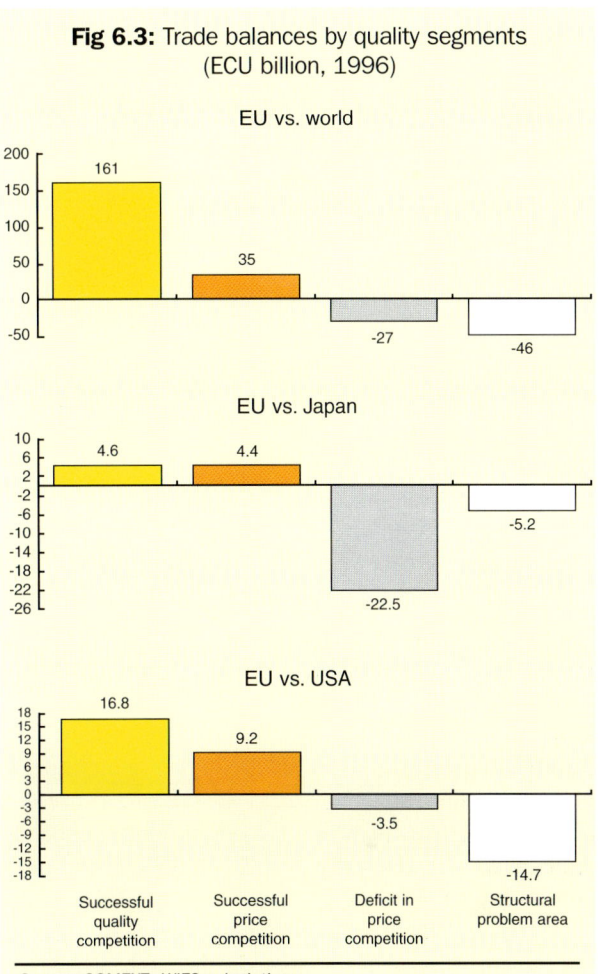

Fig 6.3: Trade balances by quality segments (ECU billion, 1996)

EU vs. world

Successful quality competition	Successful price competition	Deficit in price competition	Structural problem area
161	35	-27	-46

EU vs. Japan

Successful quality competition	Successful price competition	Deficit in price competition	Structural problem area
4.6	4.4	-22.5	-5.2

EU vs. USA

Successful quality competition	Successful price competition	Deficit in price competition	Structural problem area
16.8	9.2	-3.5	-14.7

Source: COMEXT; WIFO calculations.

Table 6.5: Trade balance in different market segments 1996

EU vs.	Successful quality competition	Successful price competition	Deficit in price competition	Structural problem area
	Quantity surplus, higher export price	Quantity surplus, lower export price	Quantity deficit higher export price	Quantity deficit lower export price
World	36 industries, e.g. Motor vehicles Machinery Air-, spacecraft	17 industries, e.g. Other chemical products	35 industries, e.g. Basic chemicals Petroleum products	7 industries, e.g. Electronic components Wearing apparel Non-ferrous metals
Japan	17 industries, e.g. Apparel Luggage, bags Textile weaving	40 industries, e.g. Basic chemicals Beverages Meat	25 industries, e.g. Motor vehicles Pharma Computer	13 industries, e.g. Special machinery Machinery Optical instruments
USA	14 industries, e.g. Vehicles Beverages	35 industries, e.g. Special machinery	35 industries, e.g. Air-, spacecraft Basic chemicals	11 industries, e.g. Computer

Source: COMEXT; WIFO calculations.

To sum up the results in a nutshell: The industries in which total EU trade is revealed to be price elastic on the one hand, and those in which it depends more on quality on the other, are approximately equal. In 52 industries, relative prices have the opposite sign to the physical quantities traded and can be labelled as the price elastic segment.

In 43 industries they have the same sign, revealing a considerable degree of quality competition. Total trade flow is larger in the quality dominated group (exports: ECU 330 billion; imports: ECU 215 billion), where the European trade surplus is generated. In the particularly price elastic industries, exports of ECU 245 billion were only slightly above the imports of ECU 237 billion in 1996.

This disaggregation reveals a rather favourable story on European external performance: the EU enjoys a trade surplus. This is largely generated by industries in which it enjoys a quantity surplus despite higher unit values, providing a rather clear indication that superior quality is the most important instrument for creating a competitive advantage. Lower prices generate a small additional surplus. A gap in price competitiveness occurs in several industries, but does not result in a large trade deficit. The structural problem area is very low.

Bilateral trade with Japan and the USA

European trade with Japan is dominated by cost advantages in Japan: in 40 industries, unit values are lower, and quantities exported are higher, generating a Japanese trade surplus of ECU 22 billion. There are also 25 industries in which Europe produces cheaper goods, but the resulting surplus is low. The same applies to the 17 industries with successful quality competition (some of them in the textiles sector). Taken with the earlier results on the high degree of specialisation in Japanese exports, the following picture emerges: Japan concentrates on high unit value industries, and uses rather low prices (or placement in the middle quality segments) to gain large surpluses in trade. However, imports remain low even when price advantages are missing or Europe offers superior quality as measured by unit values.

Bilateral trade with the USA indicates that price competition is neither creating the large surpluses, nor is it the source of major sectoral deficits. Europe has a gap in price competitiveness in 35 industries, resulting in a total deficit of only ECU 3.5 billion. Revealed price advantage in another 35 industries provides a surplus of ECU 9 billion. Larger trade imbalances in particular industries result from specialisation and non-price determinants. The segment in which Europe provides higher quality and enjoys a surplus in quantities comprises 14 industries resulting in a surplus of ECU 17 billion. Motor vehicles and beverages are the main industries in this segment. The segment in which European goods have lower unit values, but in which the trade balance is nevertheless negative, contributes a deficit of ECU 15 billion. Office machinery and computers are the major source. The overall results indicate that technological advantages and successful placement in quality segments tend to be more important determinants of trade between the USA and the EU than prices and costs.

Quality as a general industry characteristic

So far, exports from the EU to the world, and then the bilateral flows in trade with Japan and the USA, have been classified according to the relation between prices and net quantities. The four segments classified modes of competition, allowing an industry to be divided into different segments for different countries or trade flows.

In this section, the positive or negative signs revealed by the trade flows of many countries are used to classify industries as typically price elastic or quality dependent, respectively. The larger the number of opposite signs in all observed trade relations is, the greater the price elasticity should be. The higher the number of identical signs in trade flows (higher prices coinciding with higher quantities and vice versa), the higher the probability of quality as a dominant determinant of performance. This ranking of the revealed importance of quality as an industry characteristic complements the more direct quantitative estimation of price elasticities (see Box 6.4)[1].

This exercise can be performed in many variations, of which three have been chosen. For all three, the shares of bilateral trade flows in which relative prices and net quantities had the opposite sign (price elastic flows) and in which they had the same sign (non price elastic flows) were calculated. Finally, the industries were ranked according to the number of identical signs, obtaining, in this way, an indicator of the importance of non price elements.

---

[1] The method was developed in Aiginger, K., 'The use of unit values to discriminate between price and quality competition', *Cambridge Journal of Economics*, Vol. 21, 1997, pp. 571-592.

Box 6.4: Measuring price elasticities according to the Cambridge E3ME model[a]

Measuring the response of demand to price changes is a topic which is as important as it is complex. If demand changes dramatically in reaction to even minor price changes, goods are labelled as price elastic and firms use price as their main instrument to gain a competitive advantage. Costs become the crucial constraint for management since low costs are needed to undercut prices and no firm can produce at average cost higher than price in the long run.

If the product is horizontally or vertically differentiated, different specifications, locations, qualities become important and price elasticity is reduced. Specifically high wage countries have to shift to industries in which they either have a technological advantage or produce superior quality. We used unit values and the resulting quantity response to discriminate between segments in which prices and quality are the decisive determinant of success.

An alternative approach is to measure the price responsiveness with time series on prices and quantities. This approach yields a quantitative measure of the price elasticity, if the data sets are reliable and if the data include information about all the other determinants of supply and those of demand. If these are available an economic model can be estimated, which provides information about the price elasticity. If the model is sufficiently disaggregated, the price elasticity of imports and exports for different sectors and specific regions can be estimated.

The econometric model of Cambridge Econometrics includes 13 sectors within manufacturing, which roughly coincide with the NACE unrevised classification. Exports and imports are available for all EU countries with the exception of Sweden, so that a regional breakdown is possible allowing estimated elasticities for trade flows to differ across more or less developed areas. Demand is assumed to depend on technology and price and the relation is log-linear, giving elasticities which can be easily interpreted.

Limits of the analysis using trade equations alone come from the fact that partial analysis is used, that price and output data may not reflect pure changes in quantities and prices properly and that there may be omitted variables and structural breaks in the time series. Techniques available in econometrics are applied to minimise the danger of mis-specification and errors in data.

The study shows that:

- All price elasticities are relatively low, the largest export elasticities amount to 0.6, meaning that a 1% change in prices results in a 0.6% change of quantity. Average elasticities are around 0.4.

- Import price elasticities tend to be higher than export price elasticities. This fits with the finding that EU exports are sold to a larger extent on markets in which quality is more important, but imports are of lower quality-type goods and therefore to a higher degree price dependent.

- Export price elasticities are lower for the North than for the South, for the core than for the periphery and for members of the European Monetary Union than for the non-Member Countries. Import elasticities on the other hand are approximately equal across the regions. As regards individual countries, import elasticities are relatively high for Greece and the UK, implying a greater threat of competition from low cost countries.

- At industry level, the computer industry and transport equipment are price elastic while chemicals and plastics are not. While the latter finding is in line with the information from the qualitative method using unit values, the assessment for office machinery and transport is not in line with the findings by the calculation of price elasticities. This hints at the possibility that in heterogeneous industries with rapid technological change, the influence of prices and quality is particularly difficult to disentangle and econometrics and methods to detect vertical product differentiation are complementary.

[a] The study was commissioned by WIFO and performed by Cambridge Econometrics: Gardiner, B., *Analysis of EU trade-price elasticities by sector and country*, Cambridge, 1998

- Quality indicator 1: Using the EU as the reporting country, the flows vis-à-vis individual countries for all 6-digit industries (n * k flows, if n is the number of trading partners and k the number of 6-digits within an industry) were calculated. This indicator mirrors the assumption that the EU is one entity and supplies different geographical and product markets (double differentiation).

- Quality indicator 2: Using the individual member countries as reporters and total exports in each of the other 6-digit industries provides a second indicator. This indicator assumes that each country is one entity that exports to one geographical market (all partners), but in different product markets (r * k, with r as the number of EU countries) (product differentiation).

- Quality indicator 3: Using the individual member countries as reporters and all other countries as different markets, but confining the analysis to the 3-digit level, provides a third indicator. This indicator assumes that each country is an entity exporting to different geographical markets, but without product heterogeneity within the industry (geographical differentiation).

Many more possible choices exist, and none of them is an exact replica of the industrial organisation model with firms supplying well defined markets in geographical as well as product space. However, each of the chosen indicators contributes some valuable information about specific market characteristics. Together with other indicators of product differentiation and expenditures on advertising, they help us to understand the structure of markets and the respective importance of prices versus quality as determinants of the competitive process.

The ranking according to relative shares of positive signs in the quality indicators 1, 2 and 3 has been used to sort industries into three distinct groups, namely quality competition, medium price elastic industries and highly price elastic industries (allocating one third of the industries to each group). Overall, the rankings produced rather similar results.

The EU has its highest market shares in industries characterised by quality competition according to all indicators (see Table 6.6). The market shares of the price elastic industries are especially low for quality indicator 1. Under the assumption that each member country is one individual entity, it is revealed that several European countries compete as well in price elastic industries.

US market shares are above average in medium price elastic goods, while Japan has a split between industries with high emphasis on quality and those with high price elasticity.

3. Further disaggregations

Inter- vs. intra-industry trade

Rising economic development is expected to shift the predominant sources of industrial specialisation from inter-industry trade based on general factor endowments (for example in labour, physical capital or natural resources) to more differentiated intra-industry trade based on knowledge appropriation, marketing or other firm specific entrepreneurial skills.

Table 6.6 : Shares in the world market according to revealed quality competition

		EU 1989	EU 1996	Japan 1989	Japan 1996	USA 1989	USA 1996
Quality indicator 1	High	32.78	33.62	24.36	16.93	22.93	20.77
	Medium	23.34	24.06	10.67	10.01	18.44	19.07
	Low	21.88	19.03	22.71	16.09	17.73	14.99
Quality indicator 2	High	30.06	31.84	24.14	17.20	23.31	21.33
	Medium	23.48	22.66	16.81	13.79	19.51	18.49
	Low	28.21	25.18	11.52	8.95	12.77	12.76
Quality indicator 3	High	30.92	30.34	24.68	16.34	19.44	18.51
	Medium	24.71	24.54	19.32	15.69	24.18	21.41
	Low	23.21	23.22	10.84	9.74	17.56	16.48

Variables are ranked in declining order of the criteria:
High: one third of industries with highest ranks
Medium: one third of industries with medium ranks
Low: one third of industries with lowest ranks
Market share: Exports as a percentage of world imports.

Quality indicator = Number of identical signs in unit value and quantity
Q1: EU vs. countries, 6-digit level
Q2: country vs. world, 6-digit level
Q3: country vs. country, 3-digit level

Source: COMEXT, DEBA; WIFO calculations.

Inter-industry trade amounts to 43%, intra-industry trade to 57% of the EU's trade with the world. This implies that, at the level of product groups, more than half of trade occurs within the same industry. Breaking down intra-industry trade further into the predominant mode of differentiation[2], 75% appears to be vertically differentiated, while only one quarter is categorised as horizontally differentiated. Within the vertically differentiated industries, the EU lies primarily in the higher valued market segments (34% of total trade is in the higher valued segment, 13% in the lower).

In line with trade theory, more technically sophisticated industries are well represented among the industries with high intra-industry trade. Four of the ten industries with the greatest shares are engineering

---

[2] It has become a convention to use the criteria that the unit values of exports and imports do not differ by more than 15% to indicate horizontal product differentiation, whereas larger differences reveal vertical product differentiation.

industries; the largest are aircraft and spacecraft, precision instruments and medical equipment. Interestingly, horizontal differentiation dominates in each of these industries, against the general trend. Furthermore, within the vertically segmented markets, the EU is also present in the lower priced segments. The cement industry and basic chemicals are among the industries with large shares in intra-industry trade. Both are low growth and high energy-intensive industries, and cross border trade may occur.

Among the industries with low intra-industry trade, food and beverages are represented more than proportionally; steam generators is the only engineering industry in which vertical product differentiation dominates, but even here the level is low in absolute terms. In comparison with Japan and the USA, the EU concentrates its exports in industries with relatively low shares of intra-industry trade. Applying the same split of industries (based on EU trade data), the USA and Japan have larger market shares in industries with high intra-industry trade and high degrees of product differentiation.

Europe is not specialised in industries that typically have high intra-industry trade. Its market share is 28.1% in this group and 29.6% in those industries in which inter-industry trade dominates (see Table 6.7). Japan has slightly higher shares in the first group, the USA have much higher market shares in the industries in which data show high intra-industry trade.

Product differentiation

In homogenous markets, all products are sold at a unique price. However, each statistical unit (specifically those on a 3-digit industry level) comprises a large number of products, some homogenous, some of them differentiated. The variance of unit values of exports summarises the variation of prices for the same product group, as well as the variation, which arises from mixing different products in one industry. In the following, three different measures of heterogeneity are calculated: the standard deviation of the export unit value across EU countries (SD1); across the six-digit industries for EU exports (SD2); and finally the standard deviation over countries and products (SD3). The three indicators reflect different assumptions regarding the relevant markets. The first concept assumes implicitly that each European country is one economic unit, serving different regional markets. The second assumes that the EU is one firm serving different product markets, while the third implies separated products and geographical markets. The resulting indicators are positively correlated, but are far from identical.

The first indicator stresses differences in price across regions. Jewellery and nuclear fuel have large standard deviations, according to all calculations, which across regions are less than their mean, while those across products are ten times larger. Other high standard deviations across markets occur in the electronic components industry, and for audio-visual apparatus. In the pharmaceuticals, aircraft and spacecraft, ships and boats, precision instruments and optical instruments industries, standard deviation across products is much higher than across markets. In the petroleum products, pulp and paper, iron and steel, bricks, and mineral products industries, all standard deviations are very low, even compared to the low unit values in these industries. Splitting exports according to product differentiation (SD3 in Table 6.6) shows that Europe and Japan enjoy the highest market shares in industries with medium product differentiation, while the USA is specialised in industries with high product differentiation.

Table 6.7: Shares in the world market according to market characteristics

		EU 1989	EU 1996	Japan 1989	Japan 1996	USA 1989	USA 1996
Globalisation	High	25.3	24.7	22.6	16.4	20.5	18.1
	Medium	26.9	28.1	17.7	14.1	19.0	19.3
	Low	36.2	36.5	4.4	4.4	21.3	21.4
Market growth	High	26.0	25.2	23.7	17.1	23.7	20.9
	Medium	27.7	27.5	20.8	14.2	17.2	16.9
	Low	27.1	28.5	11.7	10.8	20.9	18.6
Productivity	High	29.6	31.2	21.8	16.4	23.8	21.4
	Medium	26.9	24.9	22.2	17.6	20.3	20.5
	Low	21.2	20.4	8.1	5.2	8.9	8.3
Wage level	High	28.9	30.6	21.0	16.9	24.1	22.4
	Medium	28.1	25.2	22.9	17.5	20.1	18.7
	Low	21.4	20.0	9.7	4.7	8.9	8.9
Intraindustry trade	High	29.0	28.1	18.2	14.8	25.7	21.9
	Medium	24.8	24.0	21.6	15.2	19.0	17.7
	Low	27.0	28.6	17.9	13.1	15.0	15.5
Product differentiation	High	22.9	23.1	19.1	14.8	23.3	19.8
	Medium	31.7	32.0	24.1	17.1	17.6	18.6
	Low	28.9	28.1	8.4	6.2	16.2	15.3

Industries are ranked in declining order: high-medium-low (one third with highest, medium, lowest ranks)
Globalisation: (imports + exports)/apparent consumption in the EU, Japan and the USA: extra-EU trade only.
Market growth: growth of apparent consumption in the EU, Japan and the USA.
Productivity, wage level: value added resp. wages per worker in the EU.
Intraindustry trade: share of intra industry trade (EU-world)
Product differentiation: standard deviation across markets and products of EU export unit values.

Source: COMEXT, DEBA; WIFO calculations.

Performance in globalised industries

By ranking of industries according to their exposure to international competition (calculated by the ratio of imports plus exports to apparent consumption) the following results, the following results emerge.

Office machinery, watches, and medical equipment belong to the highest globalised industries, with ratios over 75%, whereas beverages and cement are examples of low levels of global competition, with ratios of less than 25%. In contrast to Japan and the USA, the EU is characterised by high shares in world markets in industries with low globalisation. In the USA, market shares are more evenly distributed, while Japanese manufacturing is concentrated intensely in highly and moderately globalised industries, with market shares three times those of industries with low levels of globalisation.

Market growth, wage levels and productivity

When market growth is defined as the annual growth of apparent consumption in the three areas EU-Japan-USA, Japan and the USA enjoy their largest shares in the world market in high growth industries, the EU in low growth industries. Europe, as well as Japan, enjoys the largest surplus in medium growth industries, where the USA has its largest deficit. Taken together, the EU, Japan, and the USA are specialised in high growth industries, where annual growth of value added amounts to 4.3% and employment is relatively stable.

The EU enjoys its highest market share and largest trade surplus in medium wage industries. In high wage industries, the EU increased its share and has generated a considerable trade surplus. In contrast, the market shares in low wage industries are decreasing and the trade balance is marginally negative. The USA, as well as Japan, has much smaller market shares and larger trade deficits in the low wage industries. The US market share is decreasing in the high wage industries, and is stable in low wage industries.

A final disaggregation according to productivity levels reveals that the EU increased slightly its specialisation in high productivity industries and has achieved a high and increasing trade surplus. The level of specialisation of the USA in this segment decreased, resulting in a larger trade deficit. Japan has the lowest market share in the low productivity segment and a trade deficit.

4. Summary

Overall, the analysis of unit values in trade proves to be a valuable complement to the measurement of productivity. Unit values highlight the role of quality within industries and downgrade distortions in the measurement of labour productivity. This applies for example with regard to capital intensive industries, where high productivity is usually measured because of data restrictions with regard to only one input factor.

The EU specialises in more traditional industries, supplying high quality goods based on skilled and well-trained people. In many industries, the EU is a net exporter, despite higher prices.

Three sectors - machinery, motor vehicles, and chemicals - contribute more than proportionally to the large and increasing trade surplus, but inroads are also being made in more traditional industries like food, or in high tech industries, such as aircraft and spacecraft and radio, TV and communication equipment. Europe creates its trade surplus by trading with countries other than Japan and the USA, where it enjoys a quality premium of about 60%.

The deficit in trade with Japan stems from the concentration of Japanese exports in products that exhibit high unit values. Japan has abandoned exports in low productivity industries, but maintains a large share of the domestic market. Japan keeps a large part of its competitive advantage through lower prices, but in high value industries.

Trade with the USA is balanced both in value and in quantity. The USA seems to exploit competitive advantages to a lesser degree by trade, but shifts production earlier to other locations via foreign direct investment. Europe's trade with the USA does not rely on lower prices, but on mutual specialisation and competitive advantages in specific segments.

Taken as one single entity, the EU enjoys its highest market shares in industries characterised by quality competition. However, individual Member States still hold large market shares in price elastic industries.

Chapter 7
Industrial specialisation and performance

The two preceding chapters explored the structural features of internal and external performance. In this chapter, both dimensions will be re-examined with a special focus on analytical criteria considered relevant to the strategic options of firms in the creation of specific competitive advantages. A particular purpose of this chapter is to apply a new and comprehensive typology of manufacturing industries based upon their typical patterns of factor input combinations and strategic investment.

The economic rationale for the new typology is based upon the recent emphasis on irreversible investments or so called 'sunk costs' as a means of increasing differentiation and thereby moving away from pure cost competition. Sunk costs can either be exogenously determined by technology (involving investment in physical capital) or endogenously by the strategic decisions of firms to invest in intangible assets such as technological expertise or the creation of brands and goodwill[1]. The purpose of irreversible investment for example in advertising and research is to raise perceived quality and thus enhance the consumer's willingness to pay for a particular product, thereby also reducing its substitutability.

The new typology categorises industries according to the traditional factor intensities of labour and capital and additionally takes into account the inputs spent on research and development as well as advertising. By the means of statistical cluster techniques applied to US input data, a complete and mutually exclusive classification covering all manufacturing industries was created. Analytically, the novel feature of this typology is the particular choice of variables, i.e. the combination of the traditional factors of labour and capital inputs, largely reflecting exogenously given technology, to the endogenous strategic investment in advertising and innovation. Technically, the use of statistical cluster analysis provides a number of advantages relative to traditional cut-off procedures, since it represents the statistical technique specifically designed for this purpose.

1. Firm's strategies

Discriminating industries according to the broad strategic options available to firms for creating competitive advantages, a new typology categorises them according to the traditional factor intensities of labour and capital, as well as the inputs spent on research and advertising. A residual fifth category, labelled mainstream, uses factor inputs in similar proportions to total manufacturing (see Box 7.1).

In principle, objections could be raised to the classification into the four chosen dimensions. Industries always exhibit combinations of some or all these variables. In particular, the combination of high expenditures on research as well as advertising came to prominence in a similar typology by Davies-Lyons (1996)[2]. One rationale is that advertising is often modelled as a complementary activity to research and development in order to provide consumers with information when a new product is introduced to the market. This story applies easily to industries such as pharmaceuticals and optical instruments, which fall under the heading of research intensive industries as well as to detergents, games and toys or publishing, which are classified here as advertising intensive industries.

Nevertheless, the reliance on two or more distinct inputs is not unique to advertising and research but also applies equally well to the other factor inputs. For example research intensive industries repeatedly go along with high capital investment. Many of the advertising intensive industries simultaneously rely strongly on labour inputs. Actually, the cluster algorithm showed the latter two combinations of industries to be closer than advertising and research intensive industries are. Finally, no pronounced

---

[1] Sutton, J., *Sunk Costs and Market Structure*, MIT Press, Cambridge, MA, 1991.

[2] Davies, S., Lyons, B., et al., 'Industrial Organisation in the European Union', *Structure, Strategy, and the Competitive Mechanism*, Oxford University Press, Oxford, 1996.

combination of input factors emerged in the clustering process, supporting the view that each input variable spans a linearly independent dimension of its own. The following section briefly characterises the types of industries.

Particularly labour intensive industries

One quarter of manufacturing industries has been labelled as particularly labour intensive. Their share in total employment of the EU, Japan and the USA amounts to 22.1%, contrasted by a much lower share in total value added of 14.6% (see Table 7.1). Only 10.2% of the common manufacturing exports originate in this group, compared to 15.6% of total imports. Typical examples include textiles and clothing, construction materials, wood-, and metal processing.

Production techniques typically show low degrees of complexity and can rather easily be adopted in locations less endowed with manufacturing skills. Low wage countries may therefore enjoy substantial comparative advantages based on labour costs. The modest technological and organisational requirements limit the opportunities for individual enterprises to create specific competitive advantages. In economic areas characterised by high wages, substitution of labour is the logical consequence. Increasing degrees of mechanisation are typical for example in industries such as textiles, wood and metal processing.

A second means of restructuring, which is particularly important in, for example, the clothing industries, is outward processing. While parts of production migrate into low wage areas, corporate control and higher valued activities can be maintained in the home location.

Finally, suppliers of construction material, for example, build specific advantages around local user-supplier relationships, benefiting from high transportation costs, which arise from the high physical weight of their products relative to economic value.

Particularly capital intensive industries

In this subgroup only 9.9% of total manufacturing employment in the three economic areas produces 13.4% of its value added. Economies of scale support specialisation and enhance trade flows, such that this group accounts for about 17% of both total exports and imports. Typical examples are pulp and paper, refined petroleum, basic chemicals and iron and steel. These capital-intensive industries produce basic intermediate goods, which are supplied to other downstream industries. Products are typically highly homogeneous and of a commodity-like nature. Dependent on the demand of downstream manufacturing, these industries are highly exposed to fluctuations in the business cycle. As a consequence of large scale and the substantial element of sunk investment in physical capital, fluctuations in commodity prices and profits are further aggravated by sticky capacities.

Lacking opportunities for product differentiation, strategic options for individual firms most commonly include (i) a continuous process of reengineering and cost cutting, (ii) forward integration into related business activities or (iii) participation in joint ventures, mergers and take-overs, to create economies of scale and enhance strategic position as major player in the market place.

Mainstream manufacturing

Mainstream manufacturing is a residual category of 25 industries, in which input combinations did not show a pronounced reliance on any particular factor. This group accounts for about one quarter of manufacturing value added, employment and exports, but only for 15.8% of imports, when the EU, Japan and the USA are taken together. Typical examples are paper articles, plastic products, electronic equipment, motorcycles and machinery.

Although in the typical mainstream manufacturing industry production is more complex than in simple labour intensive industries, the processes involved are usually based on traditional technological regimes, mostly founded in electro-mechanical engineering.

A typical example is the machinery sector, which falls almost entirely into this group. Firm specific advantages are primarily based on bespoke developments for specific customer needs. The importance of complementary services such as planning, maintenance and training is increasing. A technically skilled workforce and the innovative upgrading of traditional technology with applications of, for example, new ICTs is essential. Close ties to downstream industries are of great importance. Thus, together with the demand for skilled labour, geographic proximity and cluster formation contribute to specific locational advantages.

Box 7.1: Factor inputs and strategic investment: the WIFO typology

The new WIFO classification groups individual industries according to their typical combinations of factor inputs, in order to reveal information about differences across industries with regard to the dominant modes of creating competitive advantage in specific marketplaces. In particular, the typology is directed towards distinction between (i) exogenously given competitive advantages based on factor endowments and (ii) endogenously created advantages based on strategic investment in intangible assets such as marketing and innovation. The new classification is based on EUROSTAT's revised NACE classification at the 3-digit level. For more details see Peneder (1998)[a].

Data and the choice of variables

The clustering process is based on the following four variables, which are designed to span four orthogonal dimensions of how to spend available units of productive inputs:

- wages and salaries
- physical capital
- advertising
- research and development

Ratios to total value added have been calculated for wages and physical capital. Expenditures on advertising and R&D are represented by their ratios to total sales. The latter are derived directly from balance sheet data. All four variables have been used in their standardised form, i.e. transformed by calculating the difference to the mean divided by the standard deviation of the variables. Data sources are DEBA (labour and capital inputs) and COMPUSTAT (advertising and R&D). Since all four dimensions of input data were available only for the USA, the clustering process is exclusively based on US-data. Correlations between the four variables are low or non-existent.

Statistical clustering

Cluster analysis classifies individual observations, depending on their relative similarity or nearness to an array of different variables. The basic idea is one of dividing a specific data profile into segments by creating maximum homogeneity within and maximum distance between groups. For the current analysis one hundred NACE 3-digit manufacturing industries are taken as observations, while the four factor inputs given above determined the discriminating variables.

A two step procedure was applied. In the first step, a non-hierarchical optimisation cluster technique, based on the iterative minimisation of within group dispersion, was used to provide a more aggregate picture of typical input combinations. For the necessary choice of a predetermined number of clusters, the following self-binding rule of thumb was used: "Choose the lowest number g that maximises the quantity of individual clusters which include more than 5% of the observed cases." (Peneder, 1995, p. 297)[b]. The outcome was g = 32 clusters, of which 9 comprise more than 5% of total observations.

In a second step, the 32 clusters from the first partition were taken as individual observations on which a hierarchical clustering algorithm was applied. This implies that no predefined number of clusters is required. Relative distances are measured, specifically focusing on similarities in patterns instead of size. In the following iterative process, clusters are formed according to the average linkage between groups, which aggregates the distances of all single pairs between an observation outside and each observation inside the cluster.

The final solution of the hierarchical clustering algorithm groups all observations into four categories, each one related to particularly high values in one of the four dimensions. After applying several variations on both (i) the measures for distance/similarity and (ii) the clustering algorithm itself no successful alternative partition to this solution emerged. Finally, a number of industries which had no particularly pronounced reliance on any of the input variables were placed in a residual category called 'mainstream' manufacturing. This more or less represents the input combination of a 'typical' 3-digit manufacturing industry.

The typology

Finally, precisely 100 NACE 3-digit manufacturing industries have been completely categorised under the following five mutually exclusive groupings of mainstream manufacturing, particularly labour-, capital-, advertising- and research intensive industries.

Like any broad classification, this new typology must be interpreted with care, since industries within these five categories are still heterogeneous and exhibit combinations of some or all these variables.

---

[a] Peneder, M., Mapping Structural Development: A New Typology of Industries Based on Labour, Capital, Advertising and R&D Inputs, WIFO, 1998, mimeo.
[b] Peneder, M., 'Cluster Techniques as a Method to Analyse Industrial Competitiveness', *IAER-International Advances in Economic Research*, Vol. I, No 3, August 1995, pp. 295-303.

Table 7.1: Shares in manufacturing: EU-Japan-USA 1996 in %

	Value added	Employment	Exports	Imports
Labour intensive	14.6	22.1	10.2	15.6
Capital intensive	13.4	9.9	16.9	17.5
Advertising intensive	22.2	22.1	10.0	14.1
Research intensive	25.3	18.6	38.8	37.0
Mainstream manufacturing	24.5	27.3	24.1	15.8
Total manufacturing	100.0	100.0	100.0	100.0

Source: DEBA, COMPET; WIFO calculations.

Particularly advertising intensive industries

This group comprises 23 industries, which together account for about 22% of total employment and value added in the three areas. This is in sharp contrast to the low shares in trade, where only 10.0% of total exports and 14.1% of total imports are generated. The low share of traded goods indicates the high importance of both local production on the one hand, and multinational investment on the other.

The most typical example is the food sector, which belongs entirely to this category. In addition, detergents and perfumes, as well as sports goods, musical instruments and games and toys, largely associated with leisure time and entertainment, fall into this category of fast moving consumer markets. Industries are often dualistic, with high quality brands on the one hand, and lower-priced, unbranded products on the other.

Strikingly characteristic of many of these industries are the easy shifts in consumer tastes. New products and temporary fashions often induce changes in preferences. Brand creation is a strategic means of differentiating products and thus reducing their substitutability. This leads to a reduction in a firm's exposure to pure cost competition. In addition, advertising stabilises the preferences of consumers.

One particular strategy is to build up integrated product lines under common brands, generating economies of scope between related products from the sharing of advertising outlays. Thus, successful brand names provide specific advantages to firms and consequently support growth strategies based on diversification as well as multinational activity.

Besides the aspect of differentiation, strategic interdependence between producers and distributors is one of the most important competitive challenges, increasingly requiring professional distribution management. Rising concentration in distribution channels is being experienced in many of these areas. The creation of brands and their support through continuous advertising is one way of reducing the producer's dependence on the retail sector. This is particularly applicable to large, primarily multinational enterprises, which are able to raise the necessary financial resources. In contrast, for small and medium sized 'no name' producers, or even for firms successfully marketing local brands, the strategic disadvantage tends to encourage joint ventures, mergers and take-overs, as efforts to counterbalance high concentration rates in the distribution networks.

Particularly research intensive industries

This grouping comprises 14 industries, which together account for 25.3% of total value added and 18.6% of total employment in the three areas. Reflecting high economies of scale, product differentiation and specialisation, research intensive goods are more highly traded than any other category. Their share in total exports and imports amounts to an outstanding 38.8% and 37.0%, respectively. Industries typically belong to one of three distinct technology fields: (i) chemicals and biotechnology; (ii) information and communication and (iii) transportation vehicles.

The nature of technological competition is highly complex and R&D efforts are a particularly risky sort of investment. Even when inventions are successfully managed in terms of technology, economic benefits are uncertain, due to their extreme dependence upon the speed and timeliness of their introduction to the market. Compensating for the higher risks, the possibility to top vertically differentiated markets induces investment in R&D through the bright prospects for higher profits. Similar to brand creation, successful innovation is a strong motivation for multinational investment.

A wide range of market failures surrounds the production and dissemination of knowledge. Probably the most serious problem concerns appropriability, since the knowledge created by innovators is exposed to imitation and diffusion by its competitors. Basically, *"a public good like knowledge remains in circulation no matter how many people consume it, and this undermines any attempt to create an artificial market"* (Geroski, 1995, p.92)[3]. The consequences threaten to undermine the proper incentives to invest in R&D.

---

[3] Geroski, P., 'Markets for technology: knowledge, innovation and appropriability', in Stoneman, P. (ed.), *Handbook of the economics of innovation and technological change*, Basil Blackwell, Oxford, 1995.

With regard to specific strategic challenges, two major themes arise: Firstly, the management of knowledge creation is a highly demanding organisational task, requiring a balance between efficient and speedy processes, while simultaneously providing room for the creative interplay of unexpected ideas. Secondly, the management of knowledge appropriation involves a number of instruments, including legal protection through patents or secrecy. Given imperfect knowledge foreclosure, it is essential that the strategy strives for lead-time and generates benefits from cumulative learning processes. For this purpose, the successful marketing of new products is an important complement to R&D.

2. Contributions to overall economic performance

In the preceding section, some major qualitative characteristics of the new industry groupings were singled out according to different strategic options for the creation of firm specific advantages. This section offers a quantitative investigation of apparent differences in terms of productivity, wage levels, unit values and growth across industry types.

Productivity and wages

The productivity of any single input factor strongly depends on the amount of complementary inputs to production. Thus, for example, high amounts of physical capital, installed to support pure labour in production, necessarily implies higher value added per employee. The same rationale extends to other (intangible) inputs as well. The underlying hypothesis therefore states that labour productivity is higher in industries where pure labour is complemented by other inputs such as physical capital, research, advertising or skills.

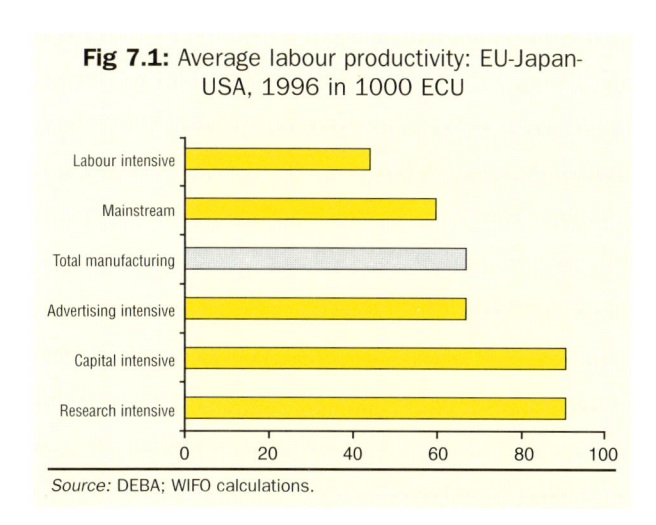

Fig 7.1: Average labour productivity: EU-Japan-USA, 1996 in 1000 ECU

Source: DEBA; WIFO calculations.

Based on a cumulative ranking of the EU, Japan and the USA according to the level of labour productivity, research- and capital intensive industries emerge highest, followed by advertising intensive industries (see Fig. 7.1). In all of them, the value of pure labour is augmented by the respective complementary inputs. Reflecting the high skills of trained workers, labour productivity in mainstream manufacturing is still higher than in labour intensive industries.

Wage levels are assumed to correspond with labour productivity. With the exception of advertising industries, where the overall wage level is lower than in the mainstream manufacturing industries, the same ranking applies as above (see Fig. 7.2).

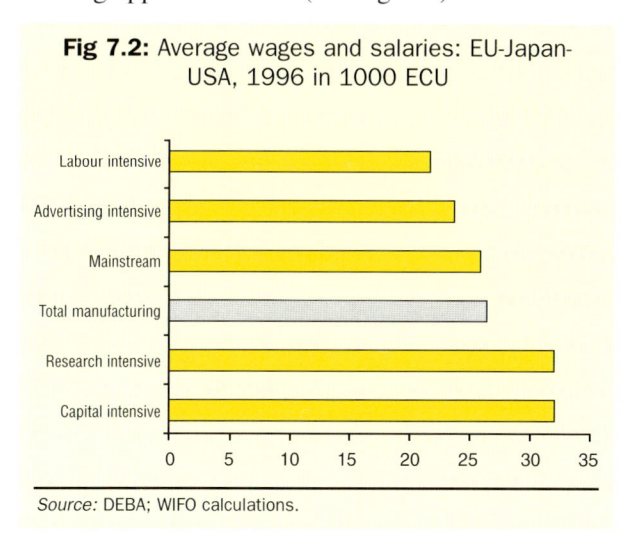

Fig 7.2: Average wages and salaries: EU-Japan-USA, 1996 in 1000 ECU

Source: DEBA; WIFO calculations.

Unit values and vertical differentiation

As with productivity (measured in nominal terms), unit values reflect the valuation of goods and services by consumers and are therefore directly linked to the potential for quality competition and vertical differentiation. Again as with productivity, unit values are not a pure and undistorted measure. The more

Box 7.2: Okun's law in a panel regression

The relationship between employment growth and output growth is investigated in a panel of industries by regressing employment growth on growth in real value added. Fixed industry and time effects control for unobserved variables which are constant over time or over industries. The panel consists of 3-digit industries in the EU, Japan, and the USA from the DEBA database provided by EUROSTAT. The estimation of fixed effects regressions produces within-group estimates. Therefore, the estimated parameter for value added growth refers to a typical industry (which emerges after correction for industry and time means). The estimated intercepts as well as the dummies for the three economic areas reflect different trends in labour productivity and/or in the capital/labour ratio. Time effects capture evenly the impact of the business cycle, to which all industries are exposed. The estimation results are summarised in Table 7.2 below.

With regard to outliers, the estimation takes a careful and restrictive approach. It includes only industries in the panel for which observations have proved valid in all three areas. Four dummies are used to control for outlying values. Additionally, ten obvious outliers have been removed. Although the panel is prone to extreme values, the estimation results are remarkably robust.

Three distinct specifications are estimated: Specification I represents the standard fixed effects model, with value added growth as well as dummies for the EU, Japan and the USA as independent variables. Specification II adds dummies for industry groups in Japan and the USA. Specification III replaces the fixed industry effects with the industry groups. The formulation of the econometric model uses the EU as a baseline, so that all coefficients referring to Japan and the USA have to be interpreted as the difference to the EU. Note that specifications II and III differ only in their definitions of the baseline: the typical EU industry is the baseline in the former, whereas the respective industry group is used as the basis for comparison in the latter case.

---

of total trade to production is again the lowest across all types of industry.

In research intensive industries, market demand moves ahead faster than in any other category and growth in value added is second only to that in the advertising intensive industries. Also exhibiting the highest rates of productivity growth and the greatest exposure to international trade, employment nevertheless decreased at a faster rate than in total manufacturing.

To sum up, the following broad generalisations can be made across the five types of industry:

- Lacking alternative options for creating competitive advantages, labour intensive industries, which produce tradable goods, are highly exposed to foreign competition on low labour costs. Despite paying the lowest wages per employee, prospects for growth in production are therefore modest.

- Capital intensive industries can afford to pay high wages because of high labour productivity. However, they are most exposed to stagnating demand and, accordingly, to large job losses across all three major economic areas.

- Exhibiting average growth dynamics, the high wages paid to skilled labour enables mainstream manufacturing to make attractive contributions to overall income creation.

- In the fast-moving consumer markets made up of advertising intensive industries, the overall economic impact has been characterised by high growth dynamics paired with outstandingly low decreases in employment during the past years.

- Finally, research intensive industries present themselves as most attractive, because of their high levels of productivity, wages and growth dynamics. In addition they are assumed to produce the most positive external effects in terms of knowledge spill-oversee to other industries and in terms of demand for sophisticated industry services.

3. Okun's law by type of industry

With respect to the analysis of the relationship between employment growth and output growth in Chapter 5, the new typology is integrated into the panel regression on Okun's law. As before, the estimated specifications are not based on a strict economic model, but rather aim only at exploring the stylised empirical relationship concerning the amount of output growth, which is necessary for stabilising employment.

The assessment of internal performance in Chapter 5 has already revealed some substantial differences in the employment intensity of value added growth between the EU, Japan and the USA (Specification I in Table 7.2). At this stage, however, the investigation can be carried one step further by introducing the differentiation across industry types into the panel regression (Specification II and III). Technical details are given in Box 7.2.

The new question under consideration is, whether or not the observed differences in the employment intensity of value added growth apply equally to all the industry types. The panel regression reveals significant differences in the employment stabilising rates of output growth between the three economic areas according to the type of industry (see Table 7.2). Relative to a typical European industry, growth of output needed to stabilise employment is particularly low in the USA for mainstream manufacturing, labour- and capital intensive industries. In Japan, capital- and advertising intensive industries exhibit a significantly lower employment stabilising rate of output growth. The most striking result is that research intensive industries exhibit no significant differences across the three economic areas.

This outcome is also reflected in the aggregated growth rates of labour productivity (see Table 7.3). In line with the process of catching up, growth in labour productivity has been higher in the EU than in the USA in all but the research-intensive industries. In contrast to the other four industry types, the USA managed to increase productivity at the same rate as the EU and even faster than Japan.

Table 7.2: Estimation results of the employment growth - output growth relationship

	Specification I		Specification II		Specification III	
	ß	t	ß	t	ß	t
Growth in value added						
Base=EU	0.37	14.42**)	0.37	14.20**)	0.39	16.86**)
USA	0.11	2.94**)	0.10	2.78**)	0.12	3.87**)
Japan	0.02	0.52	0.03	0.69	0.00	0.13
Intercept - base = EU (average of industry effects)						
Intercept - USA	1.12	5.44**)	-	-	-	-
Mainstream industries	-	-	1.87	5.50**)	1.75	4.31**)
Labour intensive	-	-	1.32	3.22**)	1.26	3.39**)
Capital intensive	-	-	1.45	2.58**)	1.37	2.36**)
Advertising	-	-	0.18	0.48	0.26	0.63
R&D intensive	-	-	0.46	0.68	0.44	0.60
Intercept - Japan	0.99	5.34**)	-	-	-	-
Mainstream industries	-	-	0.84	2.55**)	0.87	2.16 *)
Labour intensive	-	-	0.41	1.20	0.43	1.15
Capital intensive	-	-	1.86	3.12**)	1.88	2.24**)
Advertising	-	-	1.56	4.61**)	1.72	4.10**)
R&D intensive	-	-	0..42	0.64	0.47	0.64
N=66, NT=1371						
R2		0.57		0.58		0.53
Standard error of the estimate		2.98		2.96		3.07
Likelihood ratio tests for:[a]						
Fixed industry effects		167.48 (65)**)		173.72 (65)**)		
Fixed group effects						6.75 (5)
Interactions: industry-type*US				44.48 (5)**)		44.47 (5)**)
Interactions: industry-type*JP				33.40 (5)**)		34.00 (5)**)
Fixed time effects		103.25 (6)**)		103.18 (6)**)		103.18 (6)**)

Note: Time dummies and four dummies for particular high or low productivity shocks are not reported.
Estimates are corrected for heteroscedasticity.
[a] degrees of freedom in paranthesis
"**)significant at 1%; *) significant at 5%"

Source: DEBA; WIFO calculations.

Table 7.3: Average annual growth in labour productivity, 1989 to 1996

	EU	Japan	USA	EU +Japan +USA
Labour intensive	4.1	4.2	2.6	3.6
Capital intensive	3.1	3.0	1.7	3.0
Advertising intensive	4.9	3.1	2.5	3.5
Research intensive	5.0	4.1	5.0	4.8
Mainstream manufacturing	4.7	3.9	2.4	3.8
Total manufacturing	4.7	3.8	3.0	3.8

Source: DEBA; WIFO calculations.

The general implication of this finding is not immediately clear. However, this result illustrates that catching up in labour productivity is not a mechanical certainty, irrespective of the particular industry characteristics. The fact that the USA has maintained its considerable lead in research intensive industries indicates that this phenomenon is linked to the particulars of creating and appropriating technological knowledge. One thought-provoking interpretation might be that despite rapidly changing environments in dynamic markets, leads can be maintained over time and actually support the steady increase of sustainable competitive advantages. This suggests an increase in the obstacles to catching up, the more complex production technologies are. Certainly, further research into the general patterns, directions and speed of catching up processes across industries is needed, in order to draw more firm and robust conclusions on this observation.

4. Competitive performance

The purpose of the new typology is to compare performance across the three major economic areas by reference to analytical benchmarks of the underlying forces of the competitive market process. Accordingly, the strategic options available to enterprises for strengthening specific advantages are highlighted. In order to provide a comprehensive assessment of the relative strengths and weaknesses, both the relative shares of industry types in total production, as well as the export shares of each economic area in world imports, will be examined.

Table 7.4: Competitive performance by type of industry

	Share in world market			Value added shares in EU+Japan+USA		
	EU	Japan	USA	EU	Japan	USA
	1989 1996	1989 1996	1989 1996	1989 1996	1989 1996	1989 1996
			in %			
Labour intensive	28.0 25.6	11.5 9.4	10.4 9.8	35.0 35.4	28.3 28.1	36.7 36.5
Capital intensive	21.7 22.7	11.5 11.7	19.3 19.3	34.9 31.8	28.0 29.6	37.1 38.6
Advertising intensive	28.6 26.3	5.8 3.6	16.4 15.4	30.1 32.1	22.8 22.7	47.1 45.2
Research intensive	22.8 24.3	31.7 20.5	25.7 22.1	29.7 29.8	24.0 23.2	46.3 46.9
Mainstream manufacturing	40.0 37.4	23.1 17.6	21.3 21.0	34.0 34.1	27.6 27.6	38.3 38.4
Total manufacturing	27.0 26.9	19.2 14.5	20.2 18.8	32.5 32.9	25.7 25.6	41.9 41.6

Market share: Exports as a percentage of world imports.
Source: COMPET, DEBA; WIFO calculations.

With regard to overall shares in the world market, as well as in domestic production, the EU is strongest in mainstream industries (see Table 7.4), partly focusing on skill intensive sub-segments. In labour intensive industries, Europe consistently holds above average shares in value added, but below average shares in export markets. Capital and advertising intensive industries hold average shares in value added.

In the case of Japan, shares in domestic value added and world trade do not easily match. The former are much more evenly distributed, whereas the market shares of Japan's exports in world imports are highest in research intensive industries, followed by other mainstream technologies. In both cases, between 1989 and 1996, competition from emerging economies outside these three areas caused a sharp decline in market shares. Japan kept a low profile as an exporter of products from labour intensive and above all from advertising intensive industries.

In contrast to the EU, the USA is characterised by a strong - albeit in trade figures slightly eroding - position in research intensive industries, and low shares in labour intensive industries. Shares in capital intensive and other mainstream industries are broadly in line with the overall size of the economy. Advertising intensive industries exhibit high shares in domestic production, but low shares in foreign trade, indicating the particular importance of multinational activities, presumably substituting exports with foreign direct investment.

Table 7.5: Competitive performance in research intensive industries

	Share in world market			Value added shares in EU+Japan+USA		
	EU	Japan	USA	EU	Japan	USA
Industry	1989 1996	1989 1996	1989 1996	1989 1996	1989 1996	1989 1996
Agro-chemical products	74.1 67.2	12.5 5.9	51.8 31.7	27.1 30.3	13.0 11.9	59.9 57.8
Pharmaceuticals	56.5 56.1	7.1 5.4	21.8 17.4	29.7 31.3	29.2 25.9	41.1 42.8
Other chemicals	29.9 32.2	24.3 22.2	26.8 30.0	29.4 29.9	18.4 21.5	52.2 48.5
Office machinery	11.5 10.4	29.3 17.7	29.0 20.0	27.3 21.8	32.1 28.2	40.7 49.9
Electricity apparatus	35.9 37.3	31.1 25.7	22.3 21.0	47.9 45.8	23.2 25.3	28.9 28.8
Electronic components	8.8 8.9	31.9 24.3	22.8 17.4	8.9 8.6	48.4 36.0	42.7 55.4
Telecom equipment	23.9 34.4	54.1 19.4	16.8 23.1	34.7 28.9	19.0 30.7	46.3 40.4
Audio visual apparatus	7.7 10.5	42.0 17.1	9.8 10.1	30.7 27.3	62.0 65.6	7.3 7.1
Medical equipment	38.4 36.1	19.6 12.8	41.7 41.7	20.8 24.0	13.4 9.2	65.8 66.8
Precision instruments	32.8 30.5	18.7 18.5	36.2 33.2	21.6 26.2	13.1 15.0	65.2 58.8
Optical instruments	20.7 18.9	46.3 31.9	16.7 13.2	17.1 23.6	26.6 20.7	56.3 55.7
Motor vehicles	24.4 30.9	45.9 31.5	12.9 15.8	44.2 47.6	19.4 14.9	36.4 37.5
Air- and spacecraft	37.1 53.0	1.2 2.0	68.9 58.0	21.3 26.5	2.3 3.8	76.3 69.6

Market share: Exports as a percentage of world imports.
Source: COMPET, DEBA; WIFO calculations.

Focusing on research intensive industries, the EU has maintained its strong position within the research intensive branches of the chemicals sector, particularly in the fast-growing pharmaceuticals industry (see Table 7.5). At the same time, the EU gained market shares in both value added and world trade in innovative industries related to transport. In air and spacecraft, the EU considerably narrowed the gap in foreign trade, and also caught up in value added relative to the USA. In contrast, within the automobile industry, the EU won shares mainly at the expense of Japan. The EU also defended its strong position in the manufacturing of electrical machinery and control apparatus.

Partly reflecting stronger demand on world markets than on domestic markets, the EU's trade balance for the group of research intensive industries turned from a deficit of ECU 12 billion in 1989 to a surplus of ECU 27 billion in 1996. This was mainly due to improving balances in motor vehicles, pharmaceuticals and other chemicals, as well as in telecommunication equipment. The only research-intensive industries in which the trade balance deteriorated were office machinery and electronic components. The share of research intensive industries in value added remained constant.

Isolating those industries related to the information and communication technologies, the other 'non-ICT' research intensive industries show quite a favourable performance in the EU. Production in this sub-segment is growing faster in Europe than in either the USA or Japan, and trade is creating a higher surplus than in Japan, while the USA is suffering a deficit. European shares in exports are growing, and shares in value added correspond to the average of total manufacturing.

On the other hand, this split pins down the actual area of concern, namely information and communication technologies (ICTs), such as office machinery, electronic components, audio-visual apparatus, and sophisticated applications in medical equipment and precision instruments. All of these have remained either US or Japanese strongholds. It is only in the manufacturing of telecommunication equipment that the EU has shown some strength. However, in that field US leadership benefits largely from the added stimulus of rapid growth in domestic demand.

Table 7.6: Share in manufacturing exports, 1996

	Labour intensive	Capital intensive	Advertising intensive	Research intensive	Mainstream manufacturing
Belgium	12.17	26.43	13.81	27.81	19.77
Denmark	14.78	9.64	30.07	18.36	27.16
Germany	9.77	19.11	9.64	33.60	27.88
Greece	23.82	29.30	28.59	4.92	13.36
Spain	10.96	21.50	17.29	31.96	18.29
France	8.66	17.06	17.13	36.88	20.28
Ireland	3.99	13.98	21.76	51.61	8.66
Italy	20.18	13.89	15.58	16.14	34.21
Netherlands	6.15	24.87	22.34	30.09	16.55
Austria	16.13	18.43	11.70	22.76	30.98
Portugal	30.23	13.17	17.01	22.56	17.03
Finland	15.01	35.90	5.33	20.34	23.42
Sweden	11.49	25.91	5.34	33.98	23.28
United Kingdom	8.73	16.08	12.08	42.17	20.93

Source: COMEXT; WIFO calculations.

Sectoral structures within the EU exhibit a high degree of disparity (see Table 7.6). Labour- intensive industries are most prominent in the exports of Portugal, Greece and Italy. Capital intensive industries account for particularly high shares in Finland and Sweden, Belgium/Luxembourg, the Netherlands and Greece. Of all EU Member States, Italy has the highest share in mainstream manufacturing, followed by Austria, Germany and Denmark. Advertising industries contribute most to total manufacturing exports in Denmark, Greece, the Netherlands and Ireland. Research intensive industries exhibit the highest shares in Ireland, the UK, France, and to a lesser extent in Germany. However, as the data only reveal the share of research- intensive products, but not the share of a country's own innovative effort, interpretation must be careful. For example in the case of Ireland, the importance of large and recent inflows of multinational investment is particularly striking, whereas for example the more modest share in Germany may be more closely associated with new research effort.

5. Summary

To sum up, the analysis of underlying forces of competitive performance has produced the following broad picture of the EU's structural strengths and weaknesses.

Relative to Japan and the USA, industrial production in the EU exhibits the highest degree of specialisation in more traditional industries, which are still based to a large extent on labour inputs and physical capital. The EU proves its considerable technological competence and skills in mainstream manufacturing and the research-intensive industries outside the ICT sector.

Nevertheless, performance is poor compared to that of the USA and Japan in the fastest moving markets, characterised either by recent technological upturns, as in the case of ICTs, or by easily shifting consumer tastes in the advertising industries. The data suggest that the EU has missed opportunities to benefit more from the high growth dynamics in these industries, particularly when compared with the USA.

Chapter 8
Global investment and multinational firms

In the preceding chapter, the underlying forces of structural development were investigated with a strong focus on competitive advantages generated by investments in innovation and marketing. It is precisely the exploitation of these firm-specific advantages, which is commonly viewed as a major motivation for multinational activity. Alongside increasing trade volumes, multinational activity apparently is the main driving force of the globalisation process, with far-reaching influences on both the performance and structure of the economy.

Following an introductory discussion of theoretical perspectives in Section 8.1, this chapter looks at two aspects of multinational enterprises (MNEs) in the European context. In Section 8.2, a novel data set is used to describe the changing structure of European manufacturing industry between 1987 and 1993 and the role of MNEs therein. This is a micro database containing detailed information on turnover, market shares and diversification across industries, as well as on the multinationality, of the EU's leading manufacturing firms. The database is used here mainly to explore the structural implications of intra-EU multinationality. Subsequently in Section 8.3, statistics on foreign direct investment (FDI) are explored at a more aggregate level. This section investigates the inter-relationship between extra-EU multinationality and trade performance from 1989 to 1995. It compares the 5 largest EU Member States with Japan and the USA, using both descriptive statistics and an econometric model.

1. Determinants and structural impact of multinational activity

At the level of individual enterprises, the exploitation of firm specific assets (knowledge-based or derived from special organisational know-how, brands or reputation) is the most common explanation of multinational activity. In addition, constraints on growth in the firm's primary/home market often provide important push factors. The decision to set up plants abroad and become multinational is also influenced by tariff and non-tariff impediments, as well as transport costs which may render exportation a sub-optimal means of servicing foreign markets. In broad terms, this reflects proximity advantages such as easier market access and the supply of additional services, more efficient distribution systems, transportation costs proper, tariffs and non-tariff barriers to trade. On the other hand, economies of scale at plant level tend to favour exporting over multinational activities.

However, whilst the proximity/plant size trade-off is often the driving force behind the export versus foreign production decision, it does not capture the whole story. Many firms invest abroad for strategic reasons. In particular, mergers and acquisitions based on strategic motives now form an important part of FDI. Another important aspect of multinational activity lies in the specialisation within the organisation of firms. Increasingly, parts of the production process are being spread across countries within the organisation of multinational enterprises, according to the comparative advantages of home and host countries. In particular for firms located in high wage economies, this is an important strategy for remaining competitive in world markets.

The *costs* and *benefits* of multinational activity in the European context depend crucially on its motivation and on industry characteristics, as well as its impact on structural development. On the one hand, by supplementing trade, FDI might create stronger links between economies. Intra-EU FDI, in particular, may foster the European integration process. Moreover, to the extent that FDI facilitates the exploitation of comparative advantage, this should increase specialisation within the EU, resulting in pronounced structural effects on employment, productivity and growth. On the other hand, high costs, over-regulation and insufficient dynamism in the European economy might lead investors to set up plants at more favourable locations, substitute for exports and choose to supply the European market with imports.

Perhaps more importantly, the growing importance of MNEs within individual markets may sometimes be a cause of concern in *competition policy*: the very specific assets which give the MNEs their cutting edge may also result in a dampening of competition - both between incumbents and from potential entrants. If so, the expected benefits from the expansion of the European market may be constrained by the increased market shares of the leading firms, who are able to exploit market power, both at the aggregate European level and (where applicable) in national markets.

2. The multinationality of Europe's leading manufacturers[1]

Using a unique database of leading manufacturers within the EU, this section assesses the extent of and trends in (1987-1993) multinational activity, diversification and concentration in the EU (see Box 8.1). For each of nearly 100 disaggregated 3-digit industries, the 5 largest EU-producers were identified. The market shares within the EU of all such firms were estimated, as well as their production across industries and across each of the Member States. The resulting database amounts to a three dimensional matrix, in which firms' EU turnovers are disaggregated across industries, and then, within industries, across the Member States. This provides a rich source of information on the structure of individual markets, and the market shares, multinationality and diversification of individual firms. The database is available for two years, 1987 and 1993, and the sample includes about 300 firms and 96 industries in both years. During 1987 and 1993, these firms accounted for roughly one third of the entire turnover of the manufacturing sector in the EU. However, it should be remembered that the data are confined exclusively to manufacturing within the EU12.

Intra-EU multinationality

Two-thirds of these firms originate from the four largest Member States, and over 50 of the others are subsidiaries of non-EU (mainly US) MNEs (see Table 8.1). The latter statistic is testament to the significance of inward FDI from outside the EU, and the former establishes the dominant roles of Germany, France, the UK and Italy (although, the Netherlands is also an important source of a few very large firms). In 1987, these firms produced nearly 30% of their EU turnover outside of their home countries. Moreover, between 1987 and 1993 there was a pronounced increase in this intra-EU multinationality (the outside home country share rose from 30% to 37%.).

Box 8.1: The leading manufactures in the EU12.

This database is based on three criteria. First it includes all firms which can be defined as 'leading' EU manufacturers, in the sense that, measured by the scale of their turnover produced within the EU, they are amongst the largest 5 firms in at least one 3 digit manufacturing industry. Secondly, for all firms satisfying the first criterion, data were collected on their turnover in all the industries in which they operate (not only those industries in which they are 'leaders' in the above sense). Thirdly, all such estimates were compiled for both the EU as an aggregate and for all individual Member States in which the firm operates. It should be noted that (i) some firms will have non-EU parents, (ii) estimates are confined only to manufacturing operations in the EU.

The sources of the data are mainly company reports, supplemented by business directories, financial databases etc. Throughout, size is measured by the value of turnover produced in the EU. A detailed statement of the underlying data methodology can be found in Davies-Lyons, et al. (1996, Chapter 3.)

Table 8.1: Countries of origin of the EU's leading firms and their intra-EU multinationality

Country	Number of firms	1987 Total sales	% outside home country	1993 Total sales	% outside home country
Germany	64	214.0	11.5	276.5	13.9
United Kingdom	52	113.3	20.9	110.1	29.2
France	48	136.5	20.7	161.4	31.3
Italy	47	72.1	12.1	87.0	22.8
Netherlands	9	39.7	51.9	45.6	59.5
Other member states	22	16.9	20.0	25.2	25.0
Non-EU firms	53	98.4	100.0	141.6	100.0
EU	294	689.8	29.9	846.4	37.3

Two anglo/dutch firms (Unilever and Royal Dutch Shell) and the anglo/french firm (GEC/Alsthom) have been allocated 50:50 to UK, Netherlands and France respectively. Sales measured in ECU billion.

Source: Davies-Rondi-Sembenelli, 1998.

This trend of increasing intra-EU multinationality can be found in all the major Member States. From Table 8.2, it can be seen that Germany, France, the UK, Italy and Spain (in that order) are the major host countries, whilst France, Germany, the UK, the Netherlands and

---

[1] The results in this section are taken from a recently completed and updated 1993 "EU-market share matrix", produced by Rondi and Sembenelli (of CERIS-CNR, Turin) and Davies (University of East Anglia). The authors gratefully acknowledge their debt and thank for the permission to draw on this database. For more details see Davies, S.W., Rondi, L., Sembenelli, A., "Industrial Organisation in EU Manufacturing: Dynamics, 1987-93'(forthcoming as a University of East Anglia Discussion Paper, 1998).

Italy are the major sources. Non-EU based multinationals continue to account for nearly half of the inward production in manufacturing.

Multinational operations are highest in differentiated product industries, but they have also grown across the board. This underlines the importance of firm-specific assets as the main characteristic of multinational firms.

Industries most sensitive to the Single European Market have experienced some of the major increases. This confirms that the establishment of the Single European Market has led not only to an expansion of intra-EU trade volumes, but also that firms have responded by setting-up additional plants in other member countries. This is not in line with the hypothesis that multinationality is influenced by a proximity to the market / plant size trade off (since, as non-tariff barriers to trade have diminished, one might have expected that more firms would switch to exports).

The main reason for this increase in intra-EU multinational activity would appear to lie in *corporate strategy*. Firms expand production in foreign member countries for strategic reasons, for example as a response to the potential entry of new exporting firms. Multinational enterprises based outside the EU invested directly to circumvent barriers to trade and/or to participate in the further integration of the large European market. In this case trade is likely to be substituted, creating new jobs within the EU.[2]

Table 8.2: Aggregate inward and outward flows of MNEs

	Inward Production by firms originating from outside		Outward Production in other member states	
Country	1993 share of EU total	1993/1987 growth (%)	1993 share of EU total	1993/1987 growth (%)
Belgium	7.2	22.0	2.0	102.6
France	17.2	57.3	16.0	78.8
Germany	27.3	58.0	12.2	56.8
Italy	11.2	60.9	6.3	127.3
Netherlands	5.7	78.1	8.4	28.7
Spain	10.2	46.2	.	.
United Kingdom	17.1	48.3	10.2	36.0
Other member states	3.9	58.8	0.2	.
Non-EU states	.	.	44.8	45.2
EU	100.0	53.1	100.0	53.1

Two anglo/dutch firms (Unilever and Royal Dutch Shell) and the anglo/french firm (GEC/Alsthom) have been allocated 50:50 to UK, Netherlands and France respectively.

Source: Davies-Rondi-Sembenelli, 1998.

[2] Belderbos, R., Sleuwaegen, L., 'Tariff Jumping DFI and Export Substitution: Japanese Electronics Firms in Europe', *International Journal of Industrial Organisation*, Vol. XVI, No 5, 1998, pp. 601-638.

The Top 100

Comparing the joint turnover of the top 100 firms on this database between 1987 and 1993, it does not appear that this increase in intra-EU multinationality has led to an increased aggregate concentration in European manufacturing as a whole. In fact, the share of the top 100 has remained more or less constant actually, falling marginally) at roughly 30%.

This has occurred despite an increase in the index of multinationality for these firms from 2.4 to 2.87 (i.e. about 20%, see Table 8.3). The other row in the table shows part of the reason why this has *not* led to increased aggregate concentration: whilst these very large firms have increased their multinationality, they have also tended to decrease their diversification across industries.

Table 8.3: Concentration, diversification and multinationality of the top 100 firms in EU manufacturing

	1993	1987
Aggregate Concentration Share of top 100 firms (%)	28.60	29.60
Diversification index	3.95	4.34
*Intra*EU multinationality index	2.87	2.40

These indices indicate in how many countries and in how many markets a firm is typically working. Increasing entropy indices of diversification and multinationality reflect both an increasing number of industries and countries in which the firms operate, and/or growing scales of operations. The index is calculated as number equivalent of the mean entropy index, which shows how many equally sized firms would be required to produce this concentration. The entropy index is defined as:

$$-\sum_{i=1}^{n} s_i \ln s_i$$

, where s_i measures the country or industry share.
The figures shown are the arithmetic averages for the top 100.

Source: Davies-Rondi-Sembenelli, 1998.

Notwithstanding return to the core however, it is clear that the top 100 firms remain very large in terms of their aggregate sales, and that they are very often the leaders in many individual markets (see Table 8.4).

Table 8.4: The prominence of top 100 firms in individual markets, 1993

	1993
Number of top 100 firms in the top 5 in the average industry	2.6
Probability that a top 100 firm will be ranked no. x in a given 3 digit industry:	
no.1	0.59
no.2	0.57
no.3	0.55
no.4	0.45
no.5	0.42

Source: Davies-Rondi-Sembenelli, 1998.

In the typical industry 2 or 3 of the 5 market leaders come from within the top 100 firms. Indeed, in 57 of the 96 industries, the largest firm is from the top 100.

Market concentration

This leads to the key anti-trust question: has the increased multinationality of Europe's very largest manufacturers resulted in increasing concentration (and potentially market power) within individual markets? In fact, market concentration also appears to have remained more or less constant on average: in the typical industry, the top 5 firms account for 25.7% of the market (see Table 8.5). This is a one-percentage point increase compared to 1987, but this difference is not statistically significant. This is not to say, however, there are not distinct differences between types of industry - in both the level of, and changes in, concentration. 'No change on average' conceals a multitude of significant differences and changes between individual firms and industries. In particular, concentration has tended to arise in two broad types of industry: (i) where advertising is prominent, and (ii) where the EU anticipated major structural effects of the Single European Market Programme. The latter suggests that there has been an impact resulting from the establishment of the common market, where major welfare effects - besides lower prices from increased competition - were expected from the removal of market imperfections and consequent exploitation of scale economies. The former - increasing concentration in advertising industries - can be interpreted in terms of Sutton's endogenous sunk cost explanation of market structure (see Box 8.2). In these industries, concentration does not decrease as market size increases because incumbent firms invest heavily in advertising, with a resulting increase in the height of entry barriers for potential entrants.

Diversification

Returning to the top 100 firms, nearly all are significantly diversified across manufacturing industries: the average entropy index is about 4 (see table 8.3). This is a 'numbers equivalent index', which indicates that, on average, these firms spread their turnover across markets with a distribution which is arithmetically *equivalent* to operating on equal scales in four different industries. Since this index tends to weight small-scale operations only very marginally, a numerical equivalent of 4 is indicative of widespread diversification - often across up to more than 10 markets.

Nevertheless, it is the case that this diversification declined between 1987 and 1993 - albeit not drastically. Perhaps this is to be expected, bearing in mind the widespread anecdotal evidence in recent years of a 'return to core business', but it still raises an intriguing question. According to the intangible specific asset story, both R&D and advertising expenditures often form the basis of firms' competitive advantages. In many cases, these are not transferable via arm's-length trade and are best exploited by internalisation within the firm. This should apply to both diversification and multinationality, yet we have observed that, during this period, the former has tended to decrease, whilst the latter has increased strongly. Undoubtedly, this divergence deserves further analysis.

3. FDI and trade

Due to data constraints, this section must take a more aggregated, sectoral approach. It first describes the structure and trends of outward and inward FDI[3] of the five major EU-Member States, and contrasts them with the FDI-activities of Japan and the USA, in order to identify particular areas of European competitive strength. It then tests the common determinants of trade and investment in a panel regression, in order to identify whether they are primarily complements or substitutes.

Table 8.5: Change in concentration by industry type

	Mean C5 1993	1987	% change 93/87
All Manufacturing	25.7	24.5	1.2
By sensitivity to SEM			
high	32.4	29.0	3.4
medium	23.9	24.1	-0.2
low	25.0	23.5	1.5
By type of product			
Homogeneous	18.0	16.5	1.5
Differentiated			
by advertising only	25.1	22.1	3.0
by R&D only	33.6	34.2	-0.6
by both advertising and R&D	41.5	40.4	1.1

Source: Davies-Rondi-Sembenelli, 1998.

---

[3] The study uses FDI-data provided by the OECD and EUROSTAT at a sectoral level. Although the disaggregation is not detailed enough from an industrial economics perspective, it is the most comprehensive source covering inward as well as outward flows and stocks of FDI for most OECD-countries. It is possible to construct a common database with structural indicators at the same level of aggregation for the 1980s and 1990s.

Box 8.2: Multinational activity - theoretical perspectives

Starting with the work of Dunning (1994)[a] on ownership advantages, locational advantages and internationalisation, economic modelling provides two strands on the role of firm-specific assets in the relationship between multinationality and trade.

General equilibrium models

First, there is a small body of literature using general equilibrium models (e.g. Brainard, 1993, Markusen-Venables, 1995 and 1996)[b]. In the Helpman-Krugman model[c], firms expand vertically by setting up plants in low wage countries and by producing skill-intensive intermediates as well as headquarter services at the MNE's home in high wage countries. Since these models do not take transportation costs - or more general proximity advantages - into consideration, they are only able to explain one-way FDI according to a north-south type pattern. More recent approaches have introduced transportation costs, interpreted in the broad sense of advantages from proximity to the market. They can explain the widely found two-way pattern of multinational activity and trade between similarly endowed countries, depending on the trade-off between proximity advantages on the one hand and economies of scale at the enterprise and plant level on the other. The key propositions of these models are that (i) MNE activity is more intensive the more similar countries are, (ii) high trade costs tend to favour FDI over exporting - and discourage it if plant economies of scale are important and (iii) exports and MNE activity may grow complementarily over time (Pfaffermayr, 1997)[d]. Moreover, Markusen-Venables (1996), conclude that (iv) convergence in income levels between the major trading blocks (EU, USA and Japan) may be one cause of growth in multinational activities. Their model furthermore suggests that convergence in country size may not be associated with growing volumes of intra-industry trade as some of this trade is displaced by multinationals. (v) In this model the world, as a whole, benefits from multinationals, but the gains accrue disproportionately to countries which would have had more national firms in the absence of multinationals. There may also be a welfare loss for a country which would have had a large share of world industry in the absence of multinationals.

Industrial Organisation

The second strand is the Industrial Organisation literature, which takes a partial equilibrium approach, but still remains within a model structure embodying a trade off between proximity advantages and economies of scale (e.g. Horstmann-Markusen, 1992)[e]. It illustrates the commitment value of FDI in the corporate strategies of multinational firms, and, furthermore, shows that setting-up plants abroad, instead of exporting, is significantly related to market structure (causation goes both directions). In many cases, multinational activity is motivated by first mover advantages and market access, but not necessarily by cost motives. Multinational enterprises are expected to be most active in what have become known as endogenous sunk-cost industries[f]. These industries are characterised by large and escalating expenditures on advertising as well as research and development (the scales of which are endogenously determined in the oligopoly game). These endogenous sunk costs are precisely those employed to exploit the firm specific assets usually associated with MNEs.

---

[a] Dunning, J.H., *Multinational Enterprises and the Global Economy*, Addison-Wesley, Wokingham, 1994.
[b] See Brainard, S.L., 'A Simple Theory of Multinational Corporations with a Trade-off between Proximity and Concentration', *NBER-Working paper*, No 4269, 1993, Markusen, J.R., Venables, A.J., 'Multinational Firms and the New Trade Theory', *NBER-Working Paper*, No 5036, 1995, Markusen, J.R., Venables, A.J., 'The Theory of Endowment, Intra-Industry and Multinational Trade', *Centre for Economic Policy Research*, Discussion Paper, No 5036, February 1995.
[c] Helpman, E., Krugman, P., *Market Structure and Foreign Trade*, MIT - Press, Cambridge, MA, 1985.
[d] Pfaffermayr, M., *Multinational firms, trade and growth: a simple model with a trade off between proximity to the market and plant set-up costs under international trade in assets*, WIFO Working Paper, No. 90, 1997.
[e] Horstmann, I.J., Markusen, J.R., 'Endogenous Market Structures in International Trade (natura facit saltum)', *Journal of International Economics*, No 32, 1992, pp. 109-129.
[f] Sutton, J., *Sunk Costs and Market Structure*, MIT Press, Cambridge, MA, 1991.

The capacity to attract foreign direct investment benefits the EU in creating new jobs, in taking advantage of the transfer of knowledge and technology and in this way assists the ongoing structural change in European industry. On the other hand, the outward investments of European firms may foster their competitive positions and improve or initiate their access to foreign markets. Inasmuch as outward investment is based on a cost minimising strategy to relocate to low cost countries, it may also indicate lacking European attractiveness as a location of production.

FDI can take a variety of forms, including greenfield investments as well as mergers and acquisitions of existing firms. Here, the stock of FDI is measured as the book value of tangible and intangible assets held by multinational firms in foreign countries.[4]

From a conceptual point of view, the distinction between horizontal and vertical investments is particularly important (although, the data provide no information in this respect). *Horizontal investments* are presumably determined by the proximity/plant size trade-off as well as cost considerations, whereas *vertical investments* either secure supply of intermediates and materials or are market orientated to provide additional services locally. Vertical investments do not lead to a delocation of production, but may be viewed as a necessary means of increasing export performance. Horizontal foreign direct investment may relocate production, and thereby reduce employment opportunities depending on the height of trade barriers (and more generally the costs of lacking proximity to the markets), economies of scale in production and the importance of knowledge-based firm-specific assets.

Patterns of FDI and trade

Despite these limitations, FDI-data do reveal some clear trends concerning the development of FDI and trade.[5] First, in the EU5 FDI is mainly within the EU: table 8.6 shows, that in 1995, 56.6% of the FDI outflows from the EU5 countries were directed to other members of the EU. This figure is even higher without the UK, which invests heavily in the USA.

The inflows to the EU5 show a similar pattern, with 49.9% originating from EU15 countries. Again the UK, with its strong ties to the USA, is an exception.

Table 8.6: Flows of FDI: share of total FDI, 1996

	Outflows to			Inflows from		
	EU15	Japan	USA	EU15	Japan	USA
France	62.7	0.3	24.0	62.4	2.5	23.0
Netherlands	55.0	4.1	12.5	53.5	7.9	16.4
Germany	62.2	0.5	16.6	49.8	4.9	16.2
Italy	82.1	0.0	8.7	69.7	2.0	7.9
UK	34.1	0.5	47.1	19.1	0.0	84.0
EU5	56.6	0.9	23.6	49.9	3.2	32.6

Source: EUROSTAT, OECD; WIFO calculations.

Secondly, time series evidence on the relation between outward FDI-flows and GDP indicates that US firms started multinationalisation earlier than the EU15 and Japan. In the seventies (1970-1983) the average outward FDI to GDP ratio of the EU, Japan and the USA members[6] amounted to 0.5% in the USA, 0.3% in the EU, and 0.1% in Japan (see Fig. 8.1 and Table 8.7).

Fig 8.1: Flows of total outward FDI in relation to GDP, 1970-1996

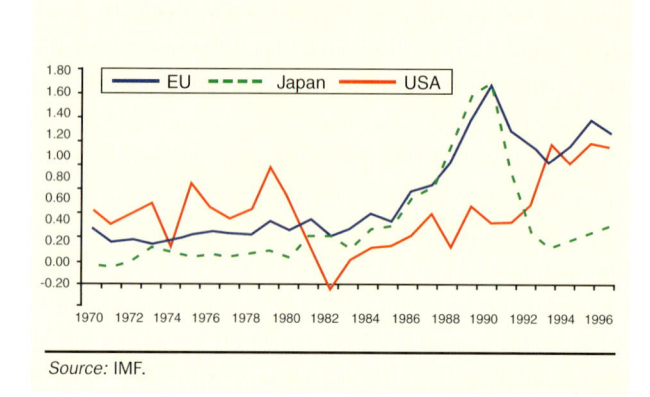

Source: IMF.

Table 8.7: Outward FDI in % of GDP

	EU	Japan	USA
Average			
1970-83	0.03	0.01	0.05
1984-91	1.02	1.00	0.47
1992-96	1.21	0.42	1.05

FDI-flows of EU include *intra*EU-FDI.

Source: EUROSTAT, OECD; WIFO calculations.

In the second half of the 1980s, multinationality accelerated significantly in the European Member

---

[4] This is only an imperfect measure of multinational activity as it is heavily affected by differences in valuation and accounting standards, but, unfortunately, data on better measures are unavailable for these purposes.

[5] For the estimations below, a consistent data set for the 5 largest EU-countries, Japan, and the USA was established. As shown in the previous section, these five Member States do account for the overwhelming majority of leading EU manufacturing MNEs.

[6] Data on aggregate FDI flows are available for the EU15 countries.

States, as well as in Japan, while the USA exhibited less dynamic growth and fell behind. During the 1993-recession, FDI-outward flows from Japan decreased significantly, but less so in the EU. The USA experienced a steady increase during this period, so that now the USA and the EU hold comparable positions.

Thirdly, in total manufacturing, the volume of FDI (now measured as inward and outward stock of FDI relative to production) and especially the volume of trade (measured as exports and imports relative to production) is considerably higher in the EU5 than in Japan and the USA (see Fig. 8.2 and Fig. 8.3). In 1995, the volume of FDI amounted to 19.0% in the EU5, compared to 13.1% in the USA and only 5.1% in Japan. For the volume of trade (including intra-EU trade), the corresponding figures are 73.3% for the EU5, 32.4% for the USA and 20.1% for Japan.

Fig 8.2: Volume of trade as share in manufacturing production: 1989-1995

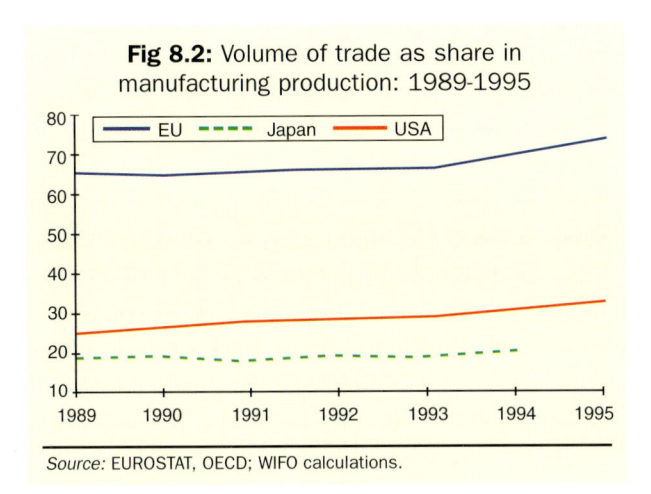

Source: EUROSTAT, OECD; WIFO calculations.

Fig 8.3: Volume of FDI as a share in manufacturing production, 1989-1995

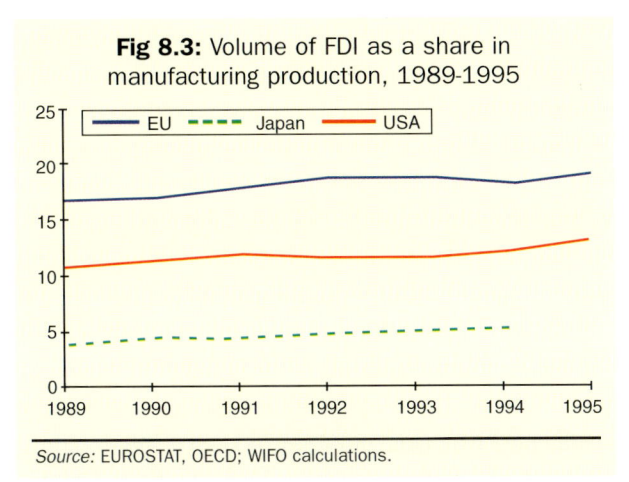

Source: EUROSTAT, OECD; WIFO calculations.

This pattern reflects proximity advantages of European countries in trade and FDI and - to a lesser extent - differences in country size. Furthermore, it underlines the important role of FDI in the European integration process. In the EU5, the outward stock outweighs inward FDI. The former increased steadily during the most recent years, whilst the latter peaked in 1992, when non-EU MNEs invested in the EU in order to take advantage of the Single European Market. The evidence suggests that the European integration process goes hand in hand with an increase in intra-EU FDI, but has not led to significant 'tariff jumping' from outside since the peak in 1992. This can also be seen in figures on FDI flows, which can be decomposed into an intra- and extra-EU component. (European Economy, 1996, p. 89).

Fourthly, in the period up to 1995, a pronounced increase in the volume of trade relative to production can be observed in the EU5 (+8.0% points) and the USA (7.5% points), whereas Japan's increase amounted to just to 1.3 percentage points. In the EU5, most of the increase took place in 1994 and 1995, perhaps as a late consequence of the Single European Market Programme. Between 1989 and 1995, the volume of FDI in relation to production grew by 2.4 percentage points in Japan, 2.4 percentage points the EU5 and 2.3 percentage points in the USA. In all three areas, this growth in the FDI volume mainly came from increased outward FDI.

For the EU5 and the USA, a simultaneous increase in the FDI balance (outward stock over inward stock) and the trade balance (exports over imports) was observed, suggesting a complementary relationship between trade and FDI (see Fig. 8.4 and Fig. 8.5).

Fig 8.4: FDI vs. trade in EU5 manufacturing: balance, 1989=100

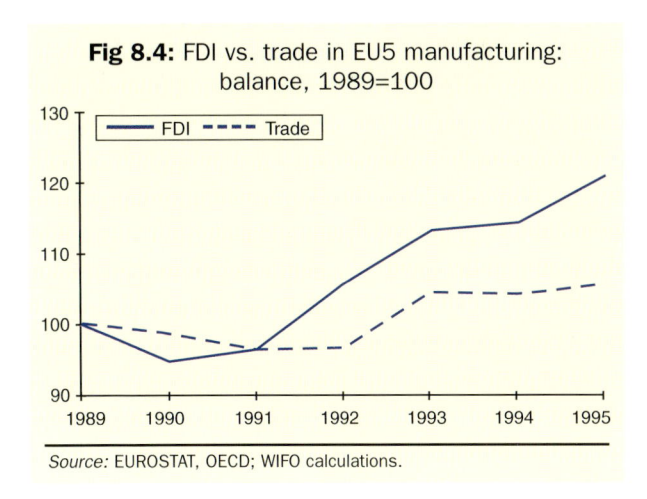

Source: EUROSTAT, OECD; WIFO calculations.

There are several reasons to expect complementarity between FDI and trade; most prominent are the large share of vertical investments, market access as a motive for FDI and the exploitation of knowledge-based firm-specific assets (see Fig. 8.6 and Fig. 8.7).

Fig 8.5: FDI vs. trade in US manufacturing: balance, 1989=100

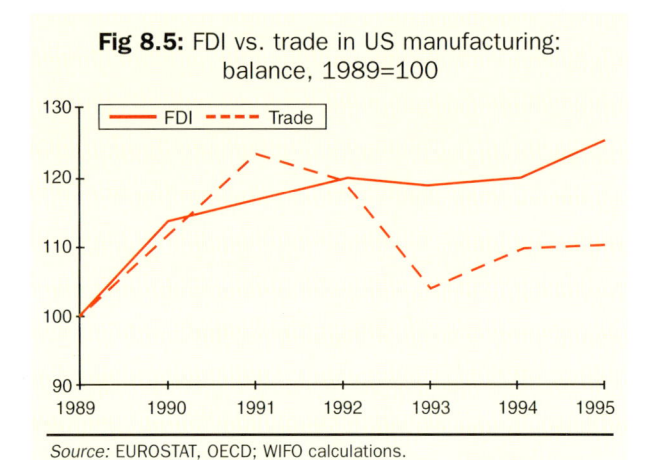

Source: EUROSTAT, OECD; WIFO calculations.

Fig 8.6: FDI vs. trade in EU5 manufacturing: volume as a share in production, 1989=100

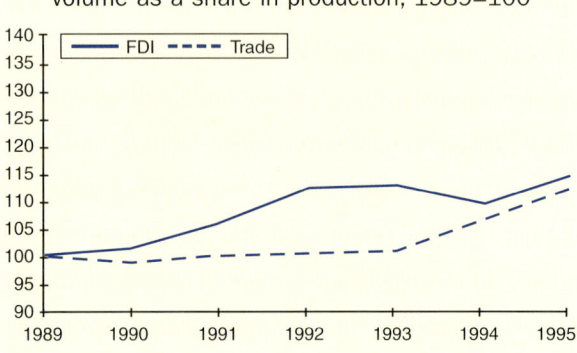

Source: EUROSTAT, OECD; WIFO calculations.

Fig 8.7: FDI vs. trade in US manufacturing: volume as share in production, 1989=100

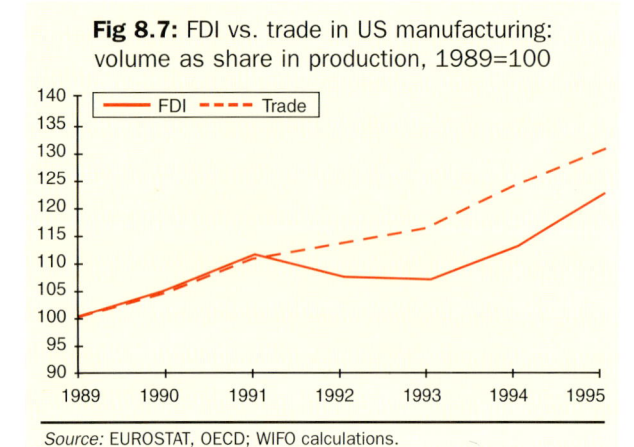

Source: EUROSTAT, OECD; WIFO calculations.

Fig 8.8: FDI vs. trade in Japanese manufacturing: volume as share in production, 1989=100

Source: EUROSTAT, OECD; WIFO calculations.

Fig 8.9: FDI vs. trade in Japanese manufacturing: balance, 1989=100

Source: EUROSTAT, OECD; WIFO calculations.

In Japan inward investment is negligible in size, reflecting restrictive policies in the past and domestic barriers against foreign direct investment. Outward FDI dominates by far. The FDI balance, however, does not seem to develop complementarily (see Fig. 8.8 and Fig. 8.9).

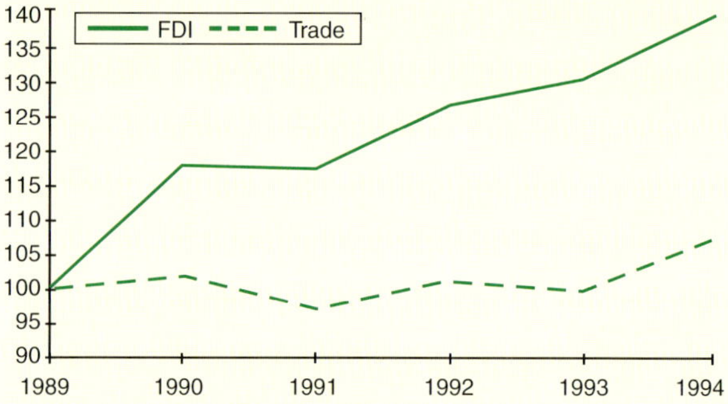

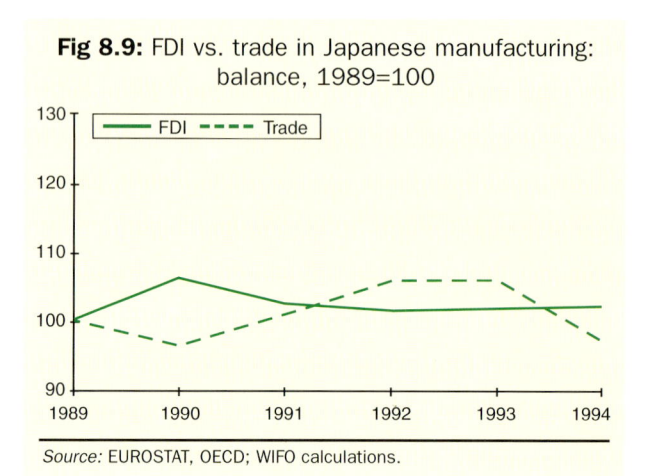

Turning to the broad sectors within manufacturing, a complicated pattern of trade and FDI emerges: Table 8.8 reports on the cross-section of industries in EU5, Japan and the USA for 1994 - the year with the most comprehensive data coverage. This shows that in the EU5 and the USA, the inward and outward FDI shares in production tend to match each other, suggesting that FDI is mainly *intra*-industry and between similarly endowed countries.

Furthermore, there is a positive correlation between trade and FDI, both between volumes and between balances. In the EU5, outward investment is higher than inward investment in all 6 sectors, with the highest balance in petroleum and chemical products, food products, metals and mechanical products. The US balance in FDI is particularly high in the vehicles and other transport equipment industry, metals and mechanical products and food products. Measured as shares in production, the EU5 FDI volume is highest in textiles and wood processing, office machinery, the petroleum industry and chemical products. In the USA the highest FDI volumes are in petroleum and chemical products, textiles, wood processing and office machinery.

Table 8.8: FDI and trade ratios at sectoral level, 1994

	Ratio of balance		Volume in % of production			
				Inward	Outward	
	FDI	Trade	FDI	FDI	FDI	Trade
EU5						
Food products	169.1	99.0	20.2	7.5	12.7	42.1
Textiles, wood activities	127.1	63.5	71.3	31.4	39.9	92.7
Metal and mechanical products	141.6	138.2	10.9	4.5	6.4	73.9
Petroleum, chemical. rubber, plastics	185.7	129.3	45.9	16.1	29.8	81.9
Information & communication equipment	108.8	81.5	58.3	27.9	30.4	165.8
Vehicles. transport equipment	131.2	109.3	11.6	5.0	6.6	78.7
Total manufacturing	157.8	108.6	18.2	7.1	11.2	69.9
JAPAN						
Food products	1 311.0	5.0	2.5	0.2	2.4	11.0
Metal and mechanical products	261.1	295.9	5.9	1.6	4.3	17.4
Total manufacturing	685.4	194.8	5.1	0.6	4.4	20.1
USA						
Food products	138.5	131.8	11.5	4.8	6.7	9.5
Textiles, wood activities	85.6	52.9	20.1	10.9	9.3	18.0
Metal and mechanical products	152.2	95.1	11.3	4.5	6.8	30.6
Petroleum, chemical. rubber, plastics	108.6	127.3	30.7	14.7	16.0	22.9
Information & communication equipment	98.5	72.0	18.4	9.3	9.1	87.6
Vehicles, transport equipment	560.5	76.1	7.2	1.1	6.1	43.0
Total manufacturing	117.3	79.1	12.1	5.6	6.5	30.8

EU5: France, Netherlands, Germany, Italy and UK. For the Netherlands and Italy, some industries are missing. Balance: ratio of stock of FDI over inward stock of FDI, exports over imports. Volumes: inward plus outward FDI stock in relation to production, exports plus imports to production. Data for 1994 are used since they were most comprehensive in their coverage.

Source: EUROSTAT, OECD; WIFO calculations.

The relationship between FDI and trade has been estimated in a panel regression combining data on FDI as well as on industry structures (see Table 8.9 and Box 8.3). Summing up the major results, significant complementarity is detected in outward activities with respect to R&D intensity, openness, average capital intensity and average firm size. However, there are also some indications of a substitutional relationship with regard to labour unit costs.

Inward activities show a substitutional relationship with respect to average firm size and an insignificant relationship with respect to labour unit costs. With respect to the proximity/plants size trade-off, there is significant substitutability. This must be interpreted with care, however, due to a possible endogeneity bias.

4. Summary

This chapter provides a number of insights into the extent and impact of multinational activities, both extra- and intra-EU. The analysis of FDI statistics demonstrates the importance of knowledge-based assets as an important common determinant of outward FDI and trade. Furthermore, FDI seems to be motivated by market access and to a lesser extent by cost considerations. In the main, FDI and trade appear to be complementary.

The analysis of firm and industry structure confirms the magnitude of the increase in intra-EU multinationality, and suggests that this is now an integral feature in the corporate structure of most large firms. Whilst it appears to have had only a minor impact, on average, on aggregate and market concentration, in some markets concentration has increased noticeably over this period. If, as seems increasingly likely, multinationality is stimulated by strategic motivation, there does exist at least a potential anti-trust dimension in some cases.

CHAPTER 8

Table 8.9: FDI and trade as shares in production, 1989 - 1995

Independent Variable	FDI-out β	t	Exports β	t	FDI-in β	t	Imports β	t
Log R&D intensity	0.4	3.8 **)	0.1	2.7 **)	-0.3	-2.7 **)	-0.1	-3.2 **)
Log average capital intensity	-0.7	-2.7 **)	-0.2	-2.8 **)	0.7	3.0 **)	0.2	2.4 **)
Log average firm size	0.9	8.6 **)	0.2	8.6 **)	0.4	2.4 **)	-0.3	-9.5 **)
Log unit labour costs	0.4	1.6 *)	-0.6	-8.9 **)	-0.2	-0.8	0.5	7.5 **)
Log openness	-0.5	-4.2 **)	0.9	22.1 **)	-1.0	-8.3 **)	1.1	27.7 **)
EU-integration dummy	-0.1	-0.5	0.1	1.6 *)	0.1	1.0	0.0	0.1
Constant	-5.4	-9.6 **)	-2.7	-12.9 **)	-8.4	-12.3 **)	1.3	5.9 **)
France	1.1	5.7 **)	0.1	2.3 **)	1.2	7.7 **)	-0.2	-2.9 **)
Netherlands	2.9	10.1 **)	0.3	3.7 **)	3.3	12.5 **)	-0.5	-4.7 **)
Germany	0.5	1.9 *)	0.4	5.5 **)	0.6	3.1 **)	-0.4	-5.9 **)
Italy	1.3	5.3 **)	0.0	0.0	0.7	4.0 **)	-0.1	-1.8 *)
UK	1.7	7.5 **)	0.1	1.9 *)	2.0	13.7 **)	-0.2	-3.0 **)
Japan	0.7	2.7 **)	-1.5	-17.3 **)	-1.8	-4.7 **)	0.0	-0.3
Textiles. wood activities	2.0	10.0 **)	0.5	7.2 **)	2.5	10.5 **)	-0.5	-7.0 **)
Petroleum.,chemical, rubber,plastics	0.7	2.2 **)	0.3	2.7 **)	2.2	8.7 **)	-0.2	-1.9 *)
Metals and mechanical products	0.5	2.5 **)	0.7	8.4 **)	1.8	7.6 **)	-0.6	-7.6 **)
Information & communication equipment	0.3	0.7 **)	0.0	-0.1	3.5	9.1 **)	0.1	0.7
Vehicles, transport equipment	-1.5	-4.5 **)	0.0	-0.4	0.8	2.6 **)	0.1	1.2
1990	0.1	0.8	0.0	-0.2	0.1	0.7	0.0	0.4 **)
1991	0.1	1.3	0.0	0.9	0.2	2.5 **)	0.0	-0.5
1992	0.2	2.3 **)	0.0	1.0	0.2	1.4	0.0	-0.7
1993	0.3	1.9 *)	0.0	0.5	0.1	0.8	-0.1	-1.4
1994	0.3	2.0 **)	0.0	0.6	0.2	1.5	-0.1	-1.6
1995	0.3	2.3 **)	0.0	0.1	0.2	1.6	0.0	-1.0
R2	0.88		0.99		0.92		0.98	
standard error of the estimate	0.38		0.11		0.36		0.11	
Heteroscedasticity	81.24	(29)	35.02	(25)	65.44	(28)	33.28	(24)
RESET	0.71		1.93*)		-5.94**)		0.08	
Normal residuals (Jarque-Bera)	6.95**)		4.37		6.29**)		4.47	

Note: Outlier dummies are skipped. Standard errors are corrected for heteroscedasticity.

*) significant at 10%
**) significant at 5%

Source: EUROSTAT, OECD, WIFO calculations.

Box 8.3: An econometric investigation of the FDI-trade relationship

Since trade and FDI are endogenously determined by common factors, these two forms of market penetration are defined as complements/substitutes with reference to variations in any exogenous variable, if they move in the same/opposite direction in the case of an exogenous change (Pfaffermayr, 1997)[a].

The vector of explanatory variables draws on the theory of FDI and trade described earlier. The share of R&D in sales and average firm size are used as rough measures of firm-specific assets. Average firm size, defined as industry output divided by the number of enterprises, also gives information on economies of scale at the enterprise level. It is positively correlated with R&D intensity. Both form proxies for knowledge-based ownership advantages. Furthermore, capital intensity (average investment relative to production) and trade openness (exports + imports relative to production) are intended to capture the proximity/size trade-off. In order to represent unit labour costs, cost differences and specialisation are included.

Data and variables

Stocks of inward and outward foreign direct investment are only available at a highly aggregated industry level (EUROSTAT, OECD; 1997). FDI-data are matched with data on trade and industry structure. A consistent data set is available for the EU5 (France, the Netherlands, Germany, Italy, UK), Japan and the USA. For the Netherlands, Italy and Japan some industries are missing. Thus, consistent data on 6 industries and 7 countries over the period 1989 to 1995 - in an unbalanced three-way panel - form the basis for the analysis of trade and FDI in this section. Since no information on stocks of intra-EU FDI is available, effects of the European integration process and the Single Market Programme can only be measured indirectly.

Econometric estimation and results

For purposes of econometric estimation, a three-way panel, with fixed country, industry and time effects is used. This gives an indication of the determinants of both FDI and trade.

Besides the explanatory variables mentioned above, the additional inclusion of industry fixed effects implies that the estimated parameters have to be interpreted as effects of within industry variation of the exogenous variables. The variation across countries, industries and over time is captured by the corresponding dummies as fixed effects. The estimated results should be interpreted as referring to the 'typical industry'.

The estimated results are largely in line with theoretical expectations: Consistent with the proximity/plant size trade-off hypothesis, trade openness, as a proxy for barriers to trade, reduces both the volume of inward and outward FDI. In the export and import equations, it is significantly positive, but some bias may remain due to endogeneity.

Both R&D intensity and average firm size are significantly positive determinants of outward FDI and exports. Inward FDI is likewise positively determined by R&D intensity, however average firm size is a negative determinant. Turning to the volume of imports, both variables have a negative impact.

Combined with the findings on average investment intensity, the results suggest that outward activities are mainly based on knowledge-specific assets and are more prominent in less capital intensive industries, whereas inward activities are more concentrated in capital intensive, but not R&D intensive industries.

The insignificance of labour unit costs as determinants of inward FDI suggests that cost considerations do not form an important motive for investment in these countries and that market orientated FDI may dominate. Outward FDI is positively related to unit labour costs at the 10% level, supporting the cost motive to some extent. In contrast, both exports and imports are heavily affected by labour unit costs exhibiting the expected signs.

There are also some interesting differences across countries and industries. Compared to the USA, outward FDI, inward FDI and export volume are all significantly higher in the EU countries, whereas import volume is lower. For outward FDI, the highest country effects are exhibited by the Netherlands, the UK, and Italy. The most export orientated countries are Germany, the Netherlands, the UK and France. Inward investment shows the highest country effects for the Netherlands, the UK, France, and the USA. The Netherlands and Germany exhibit the highest country effects in the import equation. There is also a pronounced pattern of industry effects in textiles and wood processing, exhibiting high levels in both inward and outward FDI, especially in the EU5, despite their low R&D intensity.

The evolution of trade and FDI over time is captured by time effects. However, these are only significant in the outward FDI-equation, indicating an upward trend, notably during the most recent years. In contrast, the trade equations reveal no exogenous trend.

[a] Pfaffermayr, M., *Multinational firms, trade and growth: a simple model with a trade off between proximity to the market and plant set-up costs under international trade in assets*, WIFO Working Paper, No. 90, 1997.

Chapter 9
The competitive strengths and weaknesses of European manufacturing: Summary and conclusions

The second part of the report has explored many basic facts of specialisation, structural development and competitive performance at industry level. The overall objective has been to screen the data for direct and indirect information about the competitive strengths and weaknesses of European manufacturing. The term competitiveness has been defined as the ability to raise standards of living and employment, while maintaining a sustainable environment and sustainable external balances.

1. Industry structure and competitive performance

The most important messages can be summarised as follows:

1. Intermediate specialisation of production in manufacturing industries: With the share of the manufacturing sector in total GDP amounting to 20.6%, the EU is positioned between Japan (24.7%) and the USA (18.0%). This difference in the broad patterns of specialisation is consistent with the deficit in the trade of manufacturing goods for the USA and analogously explains the aggregate trade surpluses of the manufacturing sector enjoyed in Japan and the EU

2. Global competition: As a natural consequence of faster growth in other areas, notably in the dynamic Asian countries, the total market share of the EU, Japan and the USA has declined. However, their overall trade balance is positive and increasing. This implies that the global integration of world markets and the increasing competition with low wage economies may have reduced employment opportunities in specific industries, but has not contributed to the overall decline in European manufacturing employment.

3. Favourable external balances: External balances are currently not constraining European performance. The EU enjoys larger market shares for its manufacturing exports in world imports than Japan or the USA. Despite increasing competition from emerging economies, the European market shares remained stable between 1989 and 1996. In contrast, both Japanese and US exports lost market shares in world imports. The EU's trade balance for manufacturing goods is positive and increasing.

4. European quality mark-up: The European trade surplus is generated by a quality premium in the sense that exports are more highly valued than imports. This quality premium arises primarily from trade with countries other than Japan and the USA, e.g. in Central and Eastern Europe. As a consequence of Japanese specialisation in the export of goods from high unit value industries, the unit value of European imports from Japan is twice as large as that of exports to Japan. Comparing bilateral trade flows with the USA, the number of industries in which Europe has higher or lower export unit values is roughly equal.

5. Gaps in labour productivity: Labour productivity of European manufacturing is significantly lower than that of Japan and the USA. The exact magnitude at the industry level is blurred by measurement problems, which stem in part from the interface between manufacturing and industry services. For the aggregate economy, European GDP per capita in 1997 was 14% lower than in Japan and 33% below the US level. Differences in industrial structure do not affect the European productivity gap in manufacturing, which would basically remain unaffected, if all industries were of uniform size in all the three areas.

6. Modest catching up in productivity: Labour productivity in the EU is rising faster than in the USA. Given the large initial gap, catching up is, however, progressing slowly. In past years, about one third of European productivity growth was due to structural change towards industries with higher productivity. This trend was supported by the simultaneous decline in employment shares in low productivity industries, e.g. in the clothing sector,

as well as by growing shares of high productivity industries, such as pharmaceuticals. Although productivity growth is, for the most part, still affected by general factors that apply equally across industries, catching up relative to the USA would not have been possible without structural change.

7. Growth and employment: Job creation and growth are positively related across industries in all three economic areas, but growth in manufacturing has not been high enough to stabilise employment. Between 1989 and 1996, European manufacturing matched both Japan and the USA in terms of nominal growth in value added, but performed worse in terms of employment. Econometric estimates show that the level of output growth necessary to stabilise employment is significantly lower in the USA than in the EU, which is mainly a reflection of differences in productivity growth. However, the evidence additionally suggests that European industries are more eager to rationalise production and substitute labour for capital, indicating that relative factor prices favour employment growth more in the USA than in the EU.

8. Structural pressures on employment: Relative to Japan and the USA, European manufacturing is still more specialised in labour- and capital intensive industries. Lacking alternative opportunities to create competitive advantages through product differentiation and investment in intangible assets, these industries are highly exposed to continuous cost cutting and rationalisation with a resulting substitution of labour. Thus, besides the general trends in productivity and growth, the specific industrial structure adds to the overall downward pressure on European employment.

9. Lags in fast-moving markets despite technological competence and skills: The EU proves its considerable technological competence and skills in mainstream manufacturing and the research-intensive industries outside of the information technologies. The EU is most competitive in the machinery, vehicles, and chemicals sectors, which together create a trade surplus larger than the overall surplus of the EU. However, in comparison to the USA, the low shares in total value added reveal weaknesses in innovation and marketing strategies in the most dynamic markets. European manufacturing compares poorly in the fastest moving markets, characterised either by recent technological upturns, as in the case of ICT-related research intensive industries or by easily changing consumer tastes in advertising industries.

10. European restructuring by multinational activity: European manufacturing is characterised by a significant increase in intra-EU multinational investment. Fostering the integration process and reducing regional disparities, this provides an important impetus for the ongoing restructuring of European manufacturing. This applies especially to industries relying largely on intangible firm-specific assets like innovation and marketing.

Given the lags of European manufacturing in terms of aggregate labour productivity, modest growth performance and rapidly declining employment, the sectoral analysis neither indicates overspecialisation in low productivity industries, nor a lack of technological competence and manufacturing skills. Compared to the USA, structural differences arise primarily from poor performance in creating lead-time in the fast-moving markets, where competitive advantage is based on intangible investment in research and marketing. Since first mover advantages create substantial benefits in terms of growth and employment, the USA seem to have a greater ability to benefit from the particularly high growth dynamics in these industries.

2. Economic policy

Four policy issues arising from the empirical findings deserve special attention:

11. Sectoral analysis does not imply any vertical targeting of individual industries by subsidies or strategic trade arrangements. In particular, two arguments support horizontal as opposed to vertical policies: (i) The policy of 'picking winners' generates opportunity costs relative to private market-based solutions and is subject to informational asymmetries with resulting agency problems. (ii) In addition, the analysis revealed that lower European labour productivity does not stem from structural weaknesses in the sense of being less specialised in high productivity industries than the USA.

12. Continuous upgrading of European industry: Unit labour costs in the EU are higher than in the USA, and - by a much wider margin - higher than in developing and transition countries. Low wage economies may successfully compete on price and focus on homogenous, mature products. The EU

needs to invest continuously in quality and to shift to new products at earlier stages of the product cycle. Economic policy in the EU has to promote, therefore, innovation, adaptability and the upgrading of human capital.

13. Elimination of institutional barriers: Weaknesses were identified in some dynamic markets characterised by product differentiation, marketing and innovation. The fast moving environment of these markets requires flexibility in entrepreneurial response. A prime policy target therefore is the elimination of institutional barriers to the creative and flexible management of change. Such rigidities are to be found in financial, labour and product markets, in particular in basic services, as well as in the highly disparate nature of European innovation systems.

14. European convergence and the diffusion of best practice: A high degree of disparity within the EU was found to exist for example with regard to specialisation patterns and labour productivity. An upward convergence in performance within the EU could provide a major impetus to the reduction of weaknesses observed relative to Japan and the USA. This underlines the importance of policies directed at the diffusion of best practices within the EU both in business and policy.

European Commission

The competitiveness of European industry - 1998 Report

Luxembourg: Office for Official Publications of the European Communities

1998 - 104 pp. - 21.0 x 29,7 cm

ISBN 92-828-4964-3

Price (excluding VAT) in Luxembourg: ECU 15